D1044481

ERIC LAWLOR

Looking for Osman

Eric Lawlor grew up in Ireland. He has worked on newspapers there, in England, and in the United States. The author of *In Bolivia,* Lawlor is currently completing his third travelogue. He lives in Houston, Texas.

ALSO BY ERIC LAWLOR

In Bolivia

Looking for OSMAN

Looking for OSMAN

One Man's Travels
Through the Paradox
of Modern Turkey

ERIC LAWLOR

Vintage Departures

VINTAGE BOOKS

A DIVISION OF RANDOM HOUSE, INC.

NEW YORK

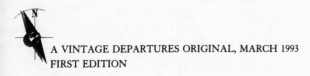

A VINTAGE DEPARTURES ORIGINAL, MARCH 1993
FIRST EDITION

Copyright © 1993 by Eric Lawlor

All rights reserved under International and Pan-American Copyright
Conventions. Published in the United States by Vintage Books, a division
of Random House, Inc., New York, and simultaneously in Canada by
Random House of Canada Limited, Toronto.

Library of Congress Cataloging-in-Publication Data
Lawlor, Eric.
  Looking for Osman: one man's travels through the paradox of modern
Turkey / by Eric Lawlor.—A Vintage departures 1st ed.
    p.   cm. — (Vintage departures)
  ISBN 0-679-73822-3 (pbk.)
    1. Turkey—Description and travel—1981–   2. Lawlor, Eric.
  I. Title.
DR429.4.L38 1993
914.96104'38—dc20   92-50090
                        CIP

BOOK DESIGN BY CATHRYN S. AISON

Manufactured in the United States of America
10 9 8 7 6 5 4 3 2 1

FOR *Sherry*

Looking for Osman

chapter 1

I hate inauspicious beginnings. One thinks of Addison disembarking at Calais and falling into the harbor; of Smollett, whose library was confiscated when he reached Boulogne; of Robert Byron, discovering, as his train left Victoria Station, that he had lost the keys to all his luggage.

My first evening in Istanbul was hardly more encouraging. I was having a drink in an outdoor café when a piece of masonry broke loose from an overhead cornice. It crashed to the pavement inches from where I was sitting.

The detonation caused a sensation: a crowd gathered, traffic halted, and those living nearby rushed to their windows. But through it all, the other patrons continued eating. Had the trajectory been only slightly different, one or more of them might have been killed, but beyond a glance at the fallen masonry and another in the direction from whence it came, the event didn't interest them. Dinner was more important.

"I hope that's not a bad omen," I said to Selim, a Turkish journalist I'd met on the plane from London. His newspaper specialized in pictures of women taking the sun on Italian beaches. His was the task of blocking out their nipples.

"Keeps you busy, does it?" I asked.

"Well, it's more complicated than it sounds," he said. "The

government keeps changing its mind. Some weeks, nipples are allowed; some weeks, they're not. It makes my job very difficult."

He made a nice impression. He was twenty-two, spoke English like a native, and wore his hair in a ponytail. He had bright pink nostrils that became red when he was angry—so red, I quite expected fire to issue from them. One of his lids drooped a little, making him look as if he were about to wink. I think that's why I warmed to him so quickly. Selim always seemed about to take one into his confidence.

For dinner, we went to a restaurant on the shores of the Bosphorus, the winding strait separating Europe and Asia. Whereas previously Selim had been somewhat shy, he now became expansive. Turks are at their best at the dinner table. They become voluble, funny, nostalgic, sentimental. Occasionally, too sentimental, said Selim. With drink taken, the Turk is apt to turn lugubrious. And when he does, he is wont to sing. Which only makes him more melancholy because Turkish songs tend to be gloomy. Songs taking so dim a view of human nature don't wonder that we're unhappy. People, they tell us, are a sorry lot. Of course our lives would be a mess.

With the exception of Selim, who said he wasn't hungry, everyone was eating with obvious enjoyment, tearing off large chunks of bread and running them over their plates, munching contentedly, gulping down wine, chattering. Their happiness made me giddy, and I ordered more kebabs. More pilaf. Another salad. I ate far too much. The next day I felt as if I'd swallowed a sheep. I—who was taught by my parents to attach no importance to food and to be wary of those who did. The French, for instance. Hadn't one of them said that, with the right sauce, he would eat his grandmother?

Turks eat with relish because their religion allows them few other indulgences. But there is another reason: their food is delicious. And not because of human ingenuity. Turkish cooking is not the result of lengthy elaboration. There are no stocks taking days to make, no overnight marinades, no sauces of infinite complexity. Turkey has no use for stocks and sauces because here everything tastes the way it should: the tomatoes like tomatoes, the cucumbers like cucumbers, the eggplants like eggplants. And the bread? Why, it might have been baked in heaven.

We ate under a plane tree in a cobbled square lined with old pine mansions with turrets and latticed windows and carved balconies. Weather-stained and needing paint, they were falling apart. Behind one of them lay a small garden. Once, odalisques would have lolled there. Filling it now was a satellite dish.

Out on the water, a ferry sounded its siren and made the sea gulls screech. Looking towards the Marmara, I could see the fortress walls the Byzantines had built; and old Stamboul, once the seat of the Ottoman Empire; and the Galata Tower guarding still the Golden Horn. There were domes everywhere. And minarets. So many, the sky bristled with them.

"I've been trying to decide why I find those minarets so moving," I said.

"And?"

"It's hard to say. They seem to be probing the sky for something. Something they aren't sure is there anymore."

Most of the diners were male. When they finished eating, they played chess and backgammon. If they had wives, they seemed in no great hurry to get home to them. The scene reminded me of Nancy Mitford's description of Oxford, where wives, she said, were superfluous, "all good talk, good food, good wine being reserved for those gatherings where there are no women."

"Turkish men seem to manage rather well without females," I suggested.

5

"We have to," said Selim, that eyelid hovering on the edge of a complicitous wink. "Islam, you know."

Selim didn't approve of Islam. Nor did he approve of sitting around in restaurants.

"Three hours is too long to spend over dinner," he said. "It's not modern."

By modern, he meant American. He had nothing but praise for America. It was his shangri-la. In America, a man who applied himself might do anything he pleased: amass a fortune, bed a starlet, occupy the White House.

"Few Americans meet a starlet, much less bed one," I said. "But if it's money you want, why can't you make it here? Start a business."

"How?" he demanded. "Where are the opportunities? The government isn't providing any. And even if it were, where would I get the capital? There is none. The country's broke. It will always be broke until we modernize."

"Isn't that what the government is doing?"

"It says it is. But very little is happening."

Like many others I would meet in Istanbul, Selim was obsessed with modernity. He worshiped Ataturk, the man who transformed this country in the 1920s. It was Ataturk who denounced the fez, the former national headdress, as "an emblem of ignorance and hatred of progress." And then he banned it. I wish he hadn't. When you alter the way a people dress, you do more than change the way they look. You change the way they see themselves. But the ban did something else: it made Turkey a lot less picturesque. When Melville visited Istanbul in 1856, the fez caps, he said, made the streets appear to be paved with tiles.

The fez disposed of, Ataturk set to work in earnest. He made his countrymen assume family names. He instituted the European weekend. He exiled the caliph. He switched to the Roman alphabet.

He banned polygamy, gave women the vote, and made it possible for them to stand for parliament. His admirers speak of him as a feminist. But was he? True, he once said that no nation can progress without its women. Yet he failed to ban the veil, a far more potent emblem of ignorance, I would have thought, than the harmless fez.

Ataturk's program was an astonishing assault on an indigenous culture, the more so for being mounted not by a colonial power but by a fervent nationalist. Such was his enthusiasm for *la vie occidentale,* his countrymen are lucky that he didn't insist on their converting to Christianity and learning French.

Selim asked if I believed in God. Drunk by now, I thought him to say, "Do you play golf?" We had a very strange conversation until I realized my error.

"Believe in God?" I said. "Yes and no."

"What does that mean?" he said, drawing on the cigar he had bought. It was a green thing, and it can't have agreed with him because beads of sweat were standing on his forehead.

"I'm an agnostic. You might say that I'm searching the world for grace."

This didn't please him at all. Ataturk hadn't believed in God, and neither should I. Ataturk said religion was "like a heavy blanket that keeps the people of Turkey asleep, that stops them from waking up, from moving forward." To repudiate God was the rational thing to do. It was modern.

"A lot of Americans believe in God," I said. It was not to address his argument, of course, but I was weary now and anxious to get to bed.

He looked surprised for a moment and then collected himself. "That proves what I've always said: you'll find reactionaries in the most advanced societies."

Selim was feeling particularly bitter just then. He had recently been denied a travel-guide license after refusing to pay a bribe.

"That sort of thing has to change," he said. "In Turkey, education and credentials mean nothing. Everything is done under the table. If you know someone, you have no problem. If you don't, bad luck."

His nostrils had become a vivid red. But while Selim might claim to deplore cronyism, he was not averse to it when he was the beneficiary. Dinner was provided free. (He knew the waiter.) And then we went to a club for raki, also free. (He knew the barman.) There was no end to the people he knew. At various times over the next few weeks, we were admitted free to cinemas, got free rides in taxis, and had free magazines thrust on us at newsstands. Once, when, like Byron, I lost the key to my backpack, a locksmith opened it and refused any payment.

"Any friend of Selim's . . . ," he said.

At 1:00 A.M., I let it slip that I was feeling tired. Actually, I was dead on my feet.

"You should have said so," said Selim. "We'll leave in an hour."

It was too late to find a taxi, so I spent the night on the floor of his apartment. Nothing in it worked. The telephone was disconnected—he had neglected to pay the bill; there was no water—the city was experiencing a drought; and the television had been broken for years—"I keep meaning to get it fixed." Several panes of glass were missing from the windows.

I fell asleep to Led Zeppelin and woke the next morning with a terrible hangover to Van Halen singing "Whipping Boy." Utter misery. I heard the song again a week later—and instantly the pain returned. We had olives for breakfast. There were pits everywhere by the time we finished, Selim preferring to spit his onto the floor. He was a great spitter.

Though he had drunk more than I had, he seemed none the worse for wear.

"You don't look well," he said. "What you need is a Turkish bath."

In *The Crescent and the Cross,* Eliot Warburton described visiting a Turkish bath, and I was keen to repeat his experience. But I almost didn't make it. Crossing a busy street, I was clipped by a car which, had it been traveling faster, might easily have killed me. (A second bad omen. And I'd been here a mere two days.)

Had this happened in New York, I'd have engaged a lawyer. But in Istanbul, drivers are always clipping people, and no one thinks any less of them for it. It is the pedestrian who is deemed to be at fault. If you find yourself in harm's way, the thinking goes, you have no one to blame but yourself.

As it had when the cornice fell, a crowd gathered when I bit the dust. Crowds are always gathering in Istanbul. What could cause such interest, I used to wonder. (This before I knew better.) Someone lying stricken? Two men come to blows? A lost child? A wounded animal? A birth? A death?

But it was rarely anything so significant. It was rarely anything at all. A man selling household gadgets, perhaps. The sort that core apples and cut glass and shell eggs—all at the same time. Or someone fishing with a length of string and a safety pin from the Galata Bridge. Turks are insatiably curious, I was forced to conclude. They will happily gape at anything.

It has been a hundred years since Warburton visited the Ottoman Empire, but the bathhouse I went to was much like the one he described. True, the fluorescent lighting jarred a little, but the ceiling of soft green and purple porcelain was much the same, and so was "the pavilion of pale-colored marble, in the center of which crystal streams leaped into an alabaster basin."

What differed was our treatment. On Warburton's arrival, he was wrapped in "softest, whitest linens" and given a pair of wooden pattens "inlaid with mother-of-pearl." I was handed what looked like an aging dishcloth, and my pattens—devoid of decoration—resembled a well-worn pair of Dr. Scholl's sandals.

(The dishcloth, by the way, is kept around the loins at all times. Turkish men link hands when they walk in public, even kiss when they meet. But this ease of manner does not extend to nudity. Islam regards the private parts with such distaste that not even members of one's own sex may be allowed to see them.)

Warburton was taken to a vaulted chamber where "cushions were laid and we were served with [water] pipes and iced sherbet." I was taken to a vaulted chamber and made to sit on a scalding bench. I had for company another man—a German, I believe—and we sat there, the two of us, gritting our teeth and not daring to say a word while our bottoms sustained third-degree burns.

There was worse to come—and it came sooner than I would have wanted in the person of a masseur. I say "person" though I can't be sure that he was one. Massive and semiclad and covered with hair, he looked less than human.

"Good God," said the German when this figure lurched towards us. "It's King Kong."

The masseur can't have liked me because, after ordering me to lie on my stomach, he proceeded to beat me. It was the kind of beating the sultan's secret police might have given an enemy of the state, and I was barely conscious when he finished. I should say *half*-finished, because he now struck me hard on the kidneys. I was being told to turn over.

Then the assault began again. If anything, it was even less enjoyable this time. I'm not sure why—unless it had to do with his pummeling my genitalia. He poked me hard in the stomach, as if testing me for doneness. No, I wasn't sufficiently tender. He resumed his exertions.

I dimly remember what happened next: more pummeling, and then I was thrown into the air a few times—like a pizza—after which I was doused in freezing water and rubbed so vigorously my tormentor may have thought he was scrubbing oysters. More dousing followed, and then, mercifully, it was over.

"Feel good?" he snarled.

I felt good, all right. Good for nothing. I hurt so much, I could barely stand.

At this stage in Warburton's ablutions, he was encouraged to recline on "silken cushions in the shaded niche of an arched window through which cool breezes, filled with orange perfumes, brushed gently over us . . . the bubbling of fountains, the singing of birds, the whispering of trees were the only sounds that met the ear."

For my part, it was suggested that I retire to a small cubicle with a bed in it and take a nap. But sleep was out of the question. I was much too tense—more tense than I'd been when I got there. If fountains bubbled and birds sang, I was not aware of them. All I could hear was the pounding in my head. My instinct now was to leave this wretched place. To leave as fast as I could. Cursing Eliot Warburton—may his shade never rest—I grabbed my clothes and fled.

There had been nothing exotic about this experience, and that was just a bit troubling because it was to find exoticism that I had come to Turkey.

"You left England to find exoticism?" said Selim when I mentioned this. "You amaze me."

"Why?"

"Isn't London exotic? Buckingham Palace? Marble Arch? Big Ben?"

"Big Ben is not exotic. Pashas waving scimitars—*that's* exotic. Beautiful odalisques lounging on divans. The tinkle of camel bells. That's what I'm here for. Oriental opulence. Decadent grandeur. All the things that make Turkey unique."

"Turkey is tired of being unique," said Selim. "We want to raise our living standards. Exoticism! What a dumb reason to go anywhere."

Perhaps it was. But Joseph Brodsky, the Nobel laureate, went to Istanbul to hear people call him Effendi. Was that any less silly? Not really. And for a very good reason. Brodsky was playing it safe. Being inspired by nonsense has its uses, he said. "It makes final disappointment so much easier to bear."

I, too, was braced for disappointment. You had to be careful with Istanbul. For centuries, people have come here expecting the pleasure domes of Xanadu. What they found was often more prosaic. Parts of Istanbul were splendid, true, but much of it—far too much—was simply nasty.

"Outwardly, it hath the fairest show.... But being entered within, there is nothing but a stinking deformity," wrote William Lithgow in 1632. Nearly two centuries later, E. D. Clarke pronounced the place more revolting than the most abominable alleys of London or Paris. It was, he said, "the meanest and poorest metropolis in the world." Henry Adams went further. "If it weren't for the beauty of the situation," he wrote in 1898, "the place would be an unredeemed hole."

In Istanbul, great expectations receded before Turkish realities. Small wonder that one visitor, enchanted by the city's silhouette, refused to leave his ship "for fear a view of the interior should dissolve the charm."

I expected disappointment for another reason. It was possible I was getting here too late. The modern era is well advanced in Turkey, and modernity is tough on the exotic. They are the mongoose and cobra of cultural history, one intent on devouring the other. Turkey has not been the same since the day in 1925 when Ataturk strolled through Kastamonu wearing not the fez decreed by tradition, but—of all things—a Panama hat. The townspeople were dumbfounded. Perhaps they realized that history was being made, that by changing hats, Ataturk had altered Turkey forever.

A lot has changed in Istanbul. A city that once relied on carrier pigeons has been invaded by the car phone. *Sunnet,* the rite of circumcision which every Moslem male must undergo, is often performed with lasers. And under the walls of Topkapi, the sprawling palace of the sultans, which is now a museum, people dance to the songs of Madonna.

For those who prize the foreignness of Istanbul, changes like these inspire a certain trepidation. "It is to feel the outlandishness of abroad that I leave home," wrote Phillip Glazebrook. "To feel the full strength of its distinctive foreign character."

Istanbul's distinctive character eluded me at first. And then I met Ercuman, an accountancy student who worked in my hotel in the evenings.

"You have to look in the right places," he said. "For a start, try the Grand Bazaar."

The bazaar made me a believer. Looking much as they did two centuries ago, its vaulted passageways weave back and forth like the splendid arabesques in Turkey's mosques. Brodsky called this place the heart, the mind, the soul of Istanbul. And one doesn't doubt it. Here, the city seems at its most uninhibited, seems most itself.

Seen from the street, its high, windowless walls give the bazaar the appearance of a giant warehouse. But go inside and you feel at once its hyperreality. The din is louder, the human clamor more intense, the press of people more urgent. It is like exploring a system of underground caverns—the high, vaulted ceilings, and the passageways, one opening off another and all lined with tiny grottoes. Four thousand shops. Two thousand ateliers. Five hundred stalls. One has the feeling of having entered another world. The light is crepuscular. Some shops sell gold. Others carpets. Silk. Silver. Samovars. Antique coins. There is the sound of brass being hammered, and the smell of spices, leather, sweetmeats. The narrow walkways are jammed. So much happening at once. The color, the noise, the crush. And all accelerated somehow. Speeded up. Faster. Ever faster.

It's hugely exhilarating, and I found myself adapting to its pace. Soon, I was bellowing like everybody else—you must if you're to make yourself heard—and pushing just as vigorously. When I emerged, I was surprised to notice that my heart was pounding and I was short of breath.

For many in this puritanical country, said Selim, commerce has become a substitute for sex. Not much of a substitute, of course, but I did wonder if he wasn't right. Certainly the sale, with its promise of eventual satisfaction, has something of the courtship ritual about it. Once the deal has been consummated, a glass of tea does duty as a postcoital cigarette.

But while the passion for commerce is still intense, it is losing some of its purity. Turkish merchants are no longer the patient suitors they were of yore, no longer the figures described by Evliya Efendi—"gowned and turbaned, sitting cross-legged behind their trays and show cases." They're more peremptory now, more aggressive, less likely to ply the prospective customer with coffee and a choice of sherbets. A love of ritual has yielded to a more craven love: the desire for quick results.

A man tried to sell me what he said was a Rolex.

"Original," he said, though I doubted it. "Two hundred dollars."

I shook my head.

"All right," he said. *"Thirty* dollars. And that's as low as I go."

The merchants aside, there is one other respect in which today's bazaar differs from earlier ones: the items being offered for sale. You'll find calculators here now. And clock radios. And jeans. And sneakers. And sweat suits. And shirts bearing the alligator insignia of Lacoste. And electric toasters. And cigarette lighters. And knickers. Lots of knickers. Dreadful things. Garments whose purpose is certainly not to lure. This clothing was designed with chastity in mind.

Chastity is splendid in its way, but there is such a thing as too much of it. Once, waiting for a ferry to take me across the Bosphorus, I sat beside a woman who promptly moved to another seat. To avoid any hint of impropriety, I suppose. It felt odd to be seen as threatening the virtue of another. It did wonders for my self-esteem. For half an hour, I was able to think of myself as a bit of a rake.

On another occasion, I was standing near a girl of ten or eleven when the wind caught her skirt and sent it billowing. The child's eyes filled with horror. *A man—and a foreigner at that— had seen her underwear.*

Istanbul is very chaste of late. Long dormant, Islam is once again astir—which may explain why the descendants of those sirens who filled the Orient of Pierre Loti and Oscar Wilde now look so dispirited.

Selim viewed this development with dismay. The government had abandoned its progressive principles, he said. It had sold out to the fundamentalists. "It could care less about modernization. All it cares about now is staying in power."

Ercuman didn't share his concern. He was a traditionalist, and the Islamic revival had his full support.

"People embrace religion when they're insecure," he said,

"and right now, Turks are very confused. The country is changing too quickly. The old values, the old traditions: they're disappearing. We don't know what to believe anymore. So we turn to God."

Ataturk was a ruthless modernizer, he said, and he had done the country only harm.

"Progress! How I hate that word. Progress is a myth. Surely people know that by now."

He was plump and balding, and he bit his lip when he felt perplexed. He bit his lip a lot.

"The West has nothing to teach us," he said. "It's vulgar and materialistic. The West should be learning from us. But what are our leaders doing? They're trying to make us another Greece. Turkey is dying. Because it's poor? No. It's dying because it wants to be rich."

I liked Ercuman. Life is of its nature hard, he said. Why try to alleviate it? We were born not to be happy but to prove ourselves, to qualify for something better in another life. A man with a generous heart, he was slow to think ill of people. When a guest—a giddy Frenchwoman—described with much merriment seeing two men hold hands, he pointed out that Turkish men often did so.

"It is natural for us," he said.

"Ah," she said, "but they were so effeminate."

"In that case," he said sadly, "there might be something in it."

If he had a failing, it was his tendency to speak in lists. Did I like English writers? he asked me once. We were walking through a street market lit entirely by kerosene lamps because a power failure had plunged the city into darkness. The vendors had on caps and open-necked shirts and suits that gleamed from too much wear. Lighted by those lanterns, their features thrown into high relief, they loomed out of the dark like figures from another age. It was breathtaking.

"English writers?" I said, only half-listening. "Yes. I like them a lot."

"Dickens and Trollope?"

"Two of the greats."

"Austen and Hardy?"

"Marvelous."

"Shakespeare?"

"Of course."

"Milton?"

At this point, I let him rattle on.

"Keats? Wordsworth? Byron?"

Even contemporary writers were familiar to him: Martin Amis, Graham Swift, Julian Barnes.

On another occasion, he inquired if I'd ever been to Brighton.

"Several times," I said.

"And Bath?"

"Yes. Bath, too."

"And Bristol? And Manchester? And Oxford? And Leeds?"

Yes, Ercuman. Yes, yes, yes. But once he started, there was no stopping him.

"And Liverpool? And Cambridge?"

Though they never met, Selim didn't like Ercuman at all. He was an arch-conservative, he said. And a Moslem fanatic, to boot. I should have nothing to do with him. He was a bad influence.

Ercuman felt much the same about Selim. People like him cared nothing for Turkey, he said. They were immoral. All they cared about was money. If I knew what was good for me, I'd stay away from him.

Each was determined that I see only *his* Turkey—the new, in Selim's case; in Ercuman's, the old.

"You know what's happening, don't you?" Ercuman said once. "We're battling for your soul."

Selim, of course, had no time for souls, but of the two of them, he was the more determined. He proposed one outing after another. First, I was invited to a meeting of the Lions Club. And when I demurred, he took me to see a play—a small amateur production of Chekhov's *The Proposal*. That such a play would be staged in Istanbul was proof, he said, that the city had joined the mainstream. It had stopped being parochial.

I didn't tell him what Chekhov said about *The Proposal*: "It's a wretched, vulgar, boring little skit, but it will go down well in the provinces. . . . I shan't put it on in St. Petersburg."

The theater was over a discotheque called The Lambada, and I was to meet him there at noon. Because I was late, I took a taxi. Selim had written the address on a slip of paper, and this I gave to the driver. He looked puzzled.

"Do you know where you're going?" I asked.

"Of course," he said, appearing to consult the address. But he can't have been able to read. He was holding it upside down.

When I reached the theater, the cast of three was in the street, drumming up business.

One of the actors carried a prop musket, which a policeman insisted on inspecting. It took him several minutes to determine that it wasn't lethal. The actor was furious, and when the policeman turned to leave, he aimed the musket at his departing back.

Selim was delighted.

"Did you see that?" he said. "The police are hated."

I didn't myself hate the police, but I had learned to be wary of them. The day before, without realizing I was outside a police station, I had removed my backpack and reached inside for a notebook. A loud click made me look up. A policeman had a rifle trained on my chest. Kurdish rebels were active in Istanbul, Ercuman told me later, and police stations were among their targets.

"I'm surprised he didn't shoot," he said.

That made *three* close shaves.

Only when the actors had mustered sufficient people to fill the twenty-five-seat theater did the play begin. Three latecomers were seated on cushions by the door.

The performance was spirited, and the all-male audience enjoyed it greatly—but in a guarded sort of way. Though the piece was played very broadly, only once did anyone laugh outright. This was the man in front of me, and he must have regretted his outburst because, pulling out a handkerchief, he pretended to be seized by a fit of coughing.

Everyone else was content to smile, and when they felt they were smiling too much—this during the really funny bits—they covered their mouths with their hands. There is a reserve about Turks I find enormously appealing.

When the play was over, the cast stood by the door and shook our hands as we left. The female lead held a small plate on which we placed donations.

Afterwards, the actors who played Chubukov and Natasha joined us for a drink. They were friends of Selim's. Like him, they were members of the new middle class and firmly Western in their outlook. In *The Proposal,* they played father and daughter; in life, they were man and wife. They invited us home for coffee.

Their apartment sported much evidence of foreign travel. There were models of the Eiffel Tower, the Acropolis, and Nelson's Column. A ceramic pig bore the legend "I love New York." They played their compact discs for me—Sinéad O'Connor, Peter Gabriel, and Bob James. Emine, the woman, showed off the suntan oil she had bought in Miami. I think she was disappointed that I wasn't more impressed.

"Miami," she repeated. "In Florida."

She was small and attractive and very intense. She smoked one cigarette after another, and when she spoke, she leaned so far forward in her chair I expected her to spring. A vein throbbed in her neck.

She and her husband supported Turkey's bid to join the European Community. But they didn't see the bid succeeding.

"Europeans look down on us," she said. "They think we're primitive."

Selim agreed. When he traveled, people were nice to him until they learned he was a Turk.

"It's never the same after that," he said. "Something changes."

All three of them seemed deeply embarrassed by the figure Turkey cuts in the world. Emine complained of being condescended to when she presented her passport at foreign airports. She said she found it mortifying. (She liked visiting the United States because Washington distinguishes between just two types of passport: United States and others.)

"What kind of coffee do you want?" she asked.

"Turkish?"

"Sorry. All I have is Maxwell House and Taster's Choice. Turkish coffee is very sweet."

"I thought Turks had a fondness for sugar. Don't you like baklava?"

She shuddered.

"People of my parents' age like baklava. My generation is different."

When I left, she made me a present of a bag of hazelnuts.

An evening later, Selim announced another excursion. We would go to the university, he said. He had a friend there. A man who worked in the philosophy department.

"You'll like him," he said. "He's a Communist."

"Is the Communist Party legal in Turkey?" I asked.

"Frankly, I don't know. No one does. The government says it is because it wants to look tolerant. But the police go on arresting people. The authorities can't seem to make up their minds."

"It's a bit like the nipples in your newspaper," I said. "It sounds to me as if Turkey's run by a lot of ditherers."

A statue of Plato stood outside the philosophy department, the brow curiously enlarged. To suggest superior intelligence, I suppose, though it had the rather odd effect of bringing to mind the creatures one sees on *Star Trek*.

Selim's friend wasn't there. Not only that. At the mention of him, the man we spoke to began to rant and rave. There was much use of the word *yok*. More than a word, *yok*. Turks have invested it with such a range of meanings, it has almost become a language. While intended to discourage, the extent of that discouragement depends entirely on the way it is uttered. A *yok* can be nothing more than a demurral, albeit a firm one. Or it can be a door slammed in your face. A *yok* can mean "I'm sorry," and it can also mean "drop dead." You can't appeal a *yok*. A *yok* is final. Categorical. Unambiguous.

To finish, the man *yok*ked several times in rapid succession, and then he turned his back on us. The audience was over.

"What was that all about?" I said when we got outside.

"He hasn't seen my friend in nearly a week," said Selim. "He said the police have been around. They want to question him."

"Because he's a Communist?"

"Maybe."

"Is that bad?"

"Very bad. In this country, people die in police custody."

He looked very worried.

"Maybe he's lying low somewhere," I said.

"Let's hope so. I'd better go and make some phone calls. Why don't I see you tomorrow?"

All a false alarm, it turned out. When Selim showed up the next morning, he was able to tell me that his friend was safe. He was in London. On holiday.

"And the police?"

"His car was stolen. They think they may have found it."

His spirits restored now, he proposed we have lunch—in McDonald's.

"Selim," I said gently. "You forget. I'm here to see the *old* Turkey."

He thought for a moment.

"OK, then. First, we'll go to McDonald's, and then I'll take you to Yedikule."

Yedikule, or the Castle of the Seven Towers, is part Byzantine, part Turkish, and overlooks the Marmara. Not a castle in the strict sense—it lacks a keep and a moat—it is more a fortified enclosure. Everywhere you turn in Turkey there are structures like this one. No country anywhere has been more coveted. No country anywhere has been more staunchly defended.

The sultans stored their treasures in Yedikule and kept prisoners in two of its towers. One of these is called the Tower of Inscriptions because those interned there carved their dolorous histories into its walls. Melville visited this place, though his journal makes scant mention of it: "Superb view of city & sea. Dungeons— Inscriptions—Soldiers—A mosque."

In the tower, the smell of misery still lingered. The smell of urine, too. Though that would be more recent. Cigarette stubs and beer cans littered the floor. Tiny cells, wet and dark, led off a stone stairway. Pigeons roosted on a catwalk.

"Imagine the conditions," said Selim, sounding very impassioned. "People had to share this place with swarming hordes of rats, with dead animals, with filth of all kinds. There were ticks to endure. And snakes. People languished in this place for years. When they emerged, they were skin and bones and covered with sores. But most of them didn't emerge. They died here and were left to rot. God! The smell must have been awful."

Clearly, he intended this as aversion therapy—a short, sharp shock that would have the effect of curing me, once and for all, of my romanticism. So this was Oriental grandeur, I was supposed to think. "Why, it wasn't grand at all. It was far from grand. It was mean and vicious." And then I'd shake my head as if waking from a long sleep, my senses finally restored.

Who knows? That's what might have happened had I just been paying more attention.

"You're looking thoughtful," said Selim.

"I'm wondering why Yedikule would sound so familiar."

We had turned to leave when it came to me. "Wait a minute," I said. "This is where Aziyadé is buried. On the other side of these walls."

"Oh, no," said Selim. He might have been Badger in *The Wind in the Willows,* deploring another of Toad's reprehensible enthusiasms. "I might have guessed. You're a fan of Loti's."

Not a fan, exactly. But I had to admit to an interest in him. The French novelist loved to travel. And he did so for reasons not unlike my own. All sorts of things set people in motion. Conrad went abroad to find romance, Melville to revive his health, and

Pietro della Valle to save his life. He was traveling, said the Roman noble, "to escape the pangs of unrequited love, an alternative to suicide."

Philip Thicknesse, the man who discovered Thomas Gainsborough, was inspired by curiosity. He wanted "to see what is to be seen." Warburton sought freedom. He felt constricted in England. He left "as men leave a crowded room, to breathe awhile, freely, in the open East." Amelia Edwards left London to find the sun. She sought out Egypt "as one might turn aside into the Burlington Arcade—to get out of the rain."

Loti and I traveled to find exoticism. A connoisseur of Oriental splendor, Loti loved Turkey, and Turkey loved him. When he died in 1923, Constantinople was plunged into mourning. Life in Turkey, he said once, was life as it should be. Only there had he ever been happy.

Of the several books he wrote about this country, the most famous is *Aziyadé*—a novel based on his affair with a Turkish woman he would later jilt. When she died in 1880 of a broken heart, Loti had a nervous breakdown, or what his doctor called a *chagrin d'amour*. Years later, he returned to Constantinople and threw himself on her grave. He kept a replica of her tombstone in his study, and when he died, he was buried with one of her scarves.

Aziyadé was the love of his life. So why did he abandon her?

Loti craved the exotic too much. (A lesson here for the likes of me.) Exoticism became his obsession, and in the end, no one place was ever exotic enough. As he left Turkey, so did he leave Senegal. And Tahiti. And India. All of them fell short. One wonders if he wasn't seeking something more than just the strange and unfamiliar. Perhaps he was seeking God.

He was a curious-looking fellow. Short and unprepossessing, he wore high-heeled shoes, curled his hair, and enlivened his face with rouge. A contemporary described him as looking like an overdressed organ-grinder. No less odd was his behavior. One of his cats he attired in a hat and skirt; another had her own calling cards; for a third, he arranged a formal baptism.

Loti isn't read anymore. Today his pathos is considered mawkish. But once, he was much admired. Anatole France liked him, as did Proust and Henry James. Loti was second rate, James admitted, but one tended not to notice—and this was his achievement. Another admirer was Sarah Bernhardt, whom he visited in her funereal bed chamber with its bat and human bones and coffin in which she was said to sleep. When the actress came to Constantinople, he took her to see the dervishes. (The dervish orders were dissolved in 1925.)

Selim didn't care to see the grave of Loti's inamorata, so I searched the narrow strip of land between Yedikule's walls and the Marmara alone. I didn't find it. The grave is no longer marked. All you'll find here now are rubbish heaps, bramble bushes, and half-expired fig trees.

My search was complicated by the small boys who followed me all afternoon. I found their attentions exhausting. Finally, though, they seemed to lose interest, and I settled down to watch the sun set. Thank God! I thought. A moment to myself. And then my blood ran cold. A head had appeared from the clump of grass in front of me. An apparition, surely. But no, for now there issued from this head a question. A question I had heard before. A question, I don't mind telling you, I had come to dread: "Do you speak English?"

The owner of the head was in his early teens. A child. You can't be rude to a child. Even if you are worn out.

"Yes, I do," I said. "Do you?"

He nodded. "My English is very good." He said this with such authority that I took him to be fluent. But, as so often happened, this proved not to be the case. In reality, his English was not "very good." It was very bad, and after a struggle, he gave up.

"Do you speak Turkish?" he asked.

I had to shake my head. No, I didn't. We had reached an impasse.

I would eventually learn some Turkish—enough to have a halting conversation—but in those early days, I felt my inadequacy keenly. I wanted to know everything about these people. But how could I if I didn't speak their language?

Warburton spoke no Turkish, either. But unlike me, he didn't mind.

"Little speech is needed for [the traveler's] few wants," he wrote. "He raises his hand, and his canvas home falls from the sumpter-horse upon the ground; the fire, the spread carpet, the light repast, all follow in their course. He waves his hand, they vanish; he points with his finger to some distant hill, or mountain pass, and his people require no other direction as to their route."

Not having "people" myself, I had to rely on gestures and facial expressions. Primitive, yes. But I had my successes. One day, I ran into a man who, a week earlier, had given me a ride to the Hilton. With him on that first occasion had been Ahmet, his ten-year-old son.

"Where's Ahmet?" I asked him.

"Off somewhere," he indicated.

"A very smart lad," I said, a sentiment he fully endorsed. "You mark my words," I added. "One of these days, that boy will be very important."

The man roared with laughter. A successful encounter, all in all. Only later did I realize that neither of us had understood a word the other said. We had communicated entirely in gestures.

Gestures, of course, are not much use on the telephone. I dreaded phoning Selim. Inserting jetons and dialing the number

I got the hang of fairly quickly. But after that, things always went awry. Had those who answered confined themselves to the words in my phrase book, there wouldn't have been a problem. But because they were all so decent, they didn't just tell me that Selim was out. They told me *why* he was out. They told me where he had gone and how he had gotten there. They told me all sorts of things, none of which I cared to hear because to none of them could I muster a response. No point in miming now. On the telephone, you can mime until you're blue in the face, and it won't do you a bit of good.

The Turks I met struggled mightily to speak English, groping for the words they wanted, looks of desperation on their faces, floundering. And the words when they came made little sense. I pretended to understand. But they weren't taken in, and the speakers would suddenly lose heart. How I felt for them. How I felt for myself. For the loss was mine as much as theirs. No, my loss was greater.

They didn't blame me for any of this. They blamed themselves. "I'm sorry," they'd say. "English not good." They seemed not to realize that it was I who was in Turkey, not they who were in England. Or maybe it didn't matter. I was a guest in this country, and they felt a duty towards me—a duty in which they now had failed.

I came to depend heavily on an old Turkish phrase book that Ercuman gave me. But it had its limitations. It contained phrases like "If you don't slow down immediately, I'll call the army" and "Your father is a general? How strange. So is mine!" Such phrases have their uses, I don't doubt, but I'd have preferred something more practical—like what to say when your tea arrives cold in the mornings. Or how to tell the maid that she mustn't touch your notes. My phrase book was silent on these subjects, its author believing, perhaps, that the traveler is not averse to cold tea and doesn't turn a hair when a week's worth of work is dispatched to a landfill.

Neither did my phrase book mention shampoo, and this was to prove a nuisance because, when my supply ran out, I had to go to a pharmacy and resort to mime. First, I poured imaginary shampoo from an imaginary bottle, and then I dried my hair— not yet imaginary, thank goodness!—with an imaginary towel. I did get my shampoo finally, but the whole thing wore me out. I could only hope that I'd never need condoms.

Without Selim to guide me, I had to find my own way home—and promptly got lost. The problem is that I discourage easily. A few short blocks, said my guidebook. So I set out. But right away, the doubts began. These blocks weren't short. And there were too many to rate as just a few. No, I must be headed in the wrong direction. Either that, or I had taken the wrong street. So I turned at the next corner. But that looked no more promising, so I turned again. And again. Until, finally, I had no idea where I was.

I'm most successful when I simply play a hunch—put my nose into the air and take off. It's when I second-guess myself that I land in trouble. Fortunately, being lost in Turkey is never very bothersome. You repair to a teahouse and order refreshments. Which was what I did now. I had just seated myself when a gypsy with a small bear asked if I'd care to take their photograph. The bear wore a muzzle. Later, I would see gypsy and bear drive by in the back of a police car. They had been arrested. Across the street, a man sold carpets in a shop still being built. "Early and unusual prices," said a sign in the window.

It's true, of course, that finding one's way in Istanbul presents special problems. The city has been around for three thousand years—ample time in which to become a jumble. And what a marvelous jumble it is: a chaotic muddle of streets that twist and turn and lead you everywhere, it seems, but where you want to go. Not like American streets—straight as a die for miles. In Istanbul, it's hard to know where you're headed because the next corner is a hundred feet away, and just beyond it is another corner, and beyond it, one more. In Istanbul, even the corners have corners.

Unable to proceed in a straight line, you proceed as best you can. Perhaps if you took this street. No, it curves too much. Maybe this one. No, this one ends in a cul-de-sac. This one, then? No, not this one, either. It does an about-turn, and now you're heading uphill when you should be heading down. Or you think you should. It's all quite baffling, and you would be right to feel aggrieved. But the odd thing is, you don't. Hear that sound? It's you. You're whistling.

I did a lot of whistling in Istanbul. The city is alien and foreign. In the space of a few hours one morning, I saw a boat filled with goats crossing the Bosphorus, and a dwarf doing handstands on a table in a teahouse. I saw an elderly artisan fashioning a pot from a sheet of tin, and a man struggling upstairs with a sheep on his back. I saw gypsies tapping tambourines, and women selling snakeskins that were said to ward off evil. I saw a water seller propped on a frayed red cushion, and sacks of spices—black and brown and crimson.

If only more places were like this. I don't approve of efforts to make the world predictable. A predictable world is a dull world. Predictability means "new towns" and genetic engineering and the kind of experiment attempted by Lenin. Instead of trying to master nature, we must learn to enjoy its mysteries.

Tea is not the only diversion when you lose yourself. You can also have your shoes shined. Istanbul has an army of wandering bootblacks, most of them young boys whose jars of polish in brass-bound boxes make them look like apothecaries in training. I hesitated to ask what those polishes contained. Until recently, the tanners in this city used dog feces to make their leathers supple. (Mexico's tanners went one better. There, D. H. Lawrence tells us, "the natives use human excrement for tanning purposes.")

My favorite bootblack was a seven-year-old I met in Eyup. His hair was shorn to the scalp, and all that polishing had dyed his hands a bluish black. He worked with touching vigor, determined to make my shoes gleam. And when he couldn't, his colleagues became involved, giving advice and offering the use of their polishes and creams.

They didn't think much of his technical skills. But that may only have been because he was more scrupulous than they were and eschewed their tricks. (I am convinced, for example, that many bootblacks treat shoes with an agent that attracts dust. Why else would footwear, just minutes after being cleaned, again look dirty?)

What was I? he wanted to know. English or German?

English, I said.

That was good, he said. Had I been German, he would have charged me 2,000 lira. Since I wasn't, he would charge me only 1,000. (Germans are disliked in Turkey for their alleged ill-treatment of Turkish guest workers.)

When I gave him a tip, his sense of honor felt compelled to reciprocate. He pulled a small plastic wallet from his pocket and removed the contents—a photograph, a stamp, something scribbled on a piece of paper.

"For you," he said, handing me the wallet. "To remind you of Turkey."

It was Ercuman who invited me to Eyup, a village on the Golden Horn. It was a Moslem shrine, he said, and he was anxious that I see it. The trip may only have been another round in his war with

Selim. But I'd begun to think there was more involved. Ercuman might have been seeking my conversion. He had recently left a copy of the Koran in my room. And just the day before, he had startled me by asking if I were circumcised.

"Why, yes," I said. "And not by laser, either. I was circumcised the old way. With a knife."

"The old way is the best way," he assured me with his usual gravity.

He was much too serious, and though I often tried to make him laugh, he resisted my best efforts. Occasionally, I'd say something that produced a glimmer of mirth. His eyes would brighten for a moment, and the corners of his mouth would twitch. But the brightness always faded, and the twitching always ceased.

"Don't you ever laugh?" I asked him once.

"Yes."

"I don't believe you."

"Of course, I laugh."

"Then laugh for me now."

Ercuman closed his eyes.

"What are you doing?"

"I'm concentrating."

But nothing came of it. Perhaps he didn't concentrate enough.

"It's hard to laugh on demand," he said.

Well, yes. I suppose it is.

In Eyup, he wanted to know if I believed in paradise. I said I considered Istanbul paradise, and this seemed to cheer him a little. Hoping to head off a discussion of the afterlife, I asked if he had ever been abroad.

"No," he said. "It's not my fate to leave Turkey."

"How can you say that? You're a young man. You might yet travel the world."

But he shook his head.

"No one in my family has ever gone anywhere. Why should I be any different?"

As he never tired of telling me, Islam means submitting to the will of God, and this he did all too gladly. For my part, I find more to admire in personal initiative, but that may only be because I don't live here. There is something about Istanbul that encourages an easy fatalism. The weight of all that history, perhaps. All that impacted time. The sense that things have been as they are for eons. It would be senseless to try to alter them. As they are now, so shall they always be.

Eyup is named for Eyup Ensari, Muhammad's standard-bearer, who is said to be buried here. His tomb, an octagonal building with a tiled interior, is a place of pilgrimage. At the door, a girl distributed lumps of sugar—in gratitude for a prayer answered, said Ercuman. I accepted mine hesitantly, not sure if her gratitude extended to an infidel like myself. But it did. As well as the sugar, she favored me with a charming smile. The pigeons were less gracious. An incontinent lot. In the hour I spent here, I was defecated on three times.

The pilgrims included a young couple married just that morning. The bride wore white, but her veil was deemed not to cover her sufficiently, and before she could enter the shrine, she had to don a scarf to shield her face. She seemed a little embarrassed by the attention she was getting. Still, working-class girl that she was, she must have realized it was unlikely to be repeated. Behind her, a stork stirred in the recesses of a plane tree.

Ercuman said couples often came to Eyup on their wedding day. And then they went to Topkapi Palace to see what remains of Muhammad: a tooth, part of a beard, a footprint. The footprint is massive—even bigger than those often ascribed to the Abominable Snowman.

If all this smacks of Moslem credulity, bear in mind that the Byzantines were little better. This city has always been a giant reliquary. By one account, St. Sophia, now known as Hagia Sophia, once contained the pillar at which Christ was scourged, the lance which pierced his side, the nails that pinned him to the cross, the crown of thorns, the manger he lay in as an infant, and the table used at the Last Supper.

In other parts of the city could be found a variety of body parts—the bones of St. Andrew, for example, the right arm of St. Stephen, the hand of St. Anne, as well as the ax employed by Noah to build the ark and the box used by Mary Magdalene to embalm the feet of Jesus. Barnum's American Museum—with its pickled prehistoric hand and a strand of Pocahontas's hair—pales by comparison.

We walked uphill to the vast cemetery that flanks Eyup. I have never seen so many graves. There were thousands and thousands of them. I tried not to tread on them, but they're so densely packed, it was hard to avoid. Many of the tombstones leaned at odd angles, and others had toppled over. There was nothing cultivated about this place: no tombs arranged in straight lines, no neatly mowed lawns, no carefully tended plots. Where the dead rested, wildflowers blossomed, and grass grew to a height of several feet. Like those who were buried here, the cemetery had returned to nature.

"Don't Moslems respect their dead?" I asked.

"Very much," said Ercuman. "But we don't make a cult of it. The dead have gone to their reward. Instead of looking after them, we rely on the dead to look after us."

An old man led us farther into the burying ground, past cypresses as tightly furled as rolled umbrellas. He was eighty, he said, and he wanted to show us where his wife was buried.

"Soon, I'll be buried with her," he said.

But I doubted it. A spry old fellow, he cleared the leaning tombstones as nimbly as any goat.

"Look," he said, pointing to the date on one of them. "Over two hundred years old."

He showed us a picture of his family: four generations, some sixty people. His face was lined like a walnut.

"Just think," said Ercuman. "When he was born, a sultan ruled this country, and Istanbul was the capital of an empire."

There were touches of that era about him still: voluminous trousers few Turks wear anymore, and a gold-embroidered waistcoat.

"He might have stepped from the last century," I said.

"Yes," said Ercuman. "He's a living link with the past."

And then the old chap had to spoil it all by taking something from his pocket. His watch had stopped, he said. Could we help him change the battery?

Later, Ercuman said that the old fellow had reminded him of Osman.

"Who's Osman?"

"You haven't heard of him? He's a legend in Istanbul. A great rogue. A scoundrel. You have to meet him."

As Ercuman described him, Osman epitomized Istanbul's freebooting ways. He was a dissembler in a city of dissemblers, a knave where knavery was king. Osman had pulled off a whole series of confidence tricks, but his most famous involved Beyazit Tower, a city landmark. Osman convinced a wealthy farmer that the tower was his. It had belonged to his family for generations. The farmer admitted to liking it. Would Osman consider selling?

Certainly not, said Osman. Why, the thing was almost an heirloom. The farmer doubled his offer, then doubled it again. And little by little, Osman began to yield. But he did so grudgingly.

When his father found out, said Osman, he expected to be disowned.

"Where is Osman now?" I said.

"Let me make some inquiries," said Ercuman. "I haven't heard him mentioned in a while. He may have retired. I'll ask around."

While we waited for a ferry to take us home, a baby cried. At first, people pretended not to notice. But when it persisted, an embarrassed silence fell. And then the women began to mutter.

"This is too much."

"This is not how babies should behave."

The mother, young and inexperienced, began to panic. To muffle its screams, she pressed the baby to her chest. But for Ercuman, it might have suffocated. Scooping up the howling child, he rocked it in his arms until it fell asleep.

It was getting dark when we edged down the Golden Horn. The horn is much diminished. Gone are its palaces and summer houses, its gardens and wooded glades. Its waters are fetid now, its banks lined with shipyards and tiny factories. But I hardly noticed. In the distance was the Stamboul skyline, its spires burnished by the setting sun, its domes looking like a family of sea turtles briefly come ashore. The scene was spectral. Too beautiful to be real. Had it disappeared suddenly, I wouldn't have batted an eye.

In the dwindling purple light, the city seemed to crumple, its seven hills drawing closer together. It looked more beautiful than I'd ever seen it. Hagia Sophia, once the most important church in Christendom; the Blue Mosque, famous for its tile; Topkapi Palace, where the sultans played. . . . This skyline didn't inspire lofty thoughts. It produced a feeling of utter calm—the tranquillity one feels, the complete surrender, in the presence of something so apt, so absolutely right, that to alter a single detail would be to ruin it completely.

I didn't sleep that night. The Poles in the next room were having a party. They were smugglers. Engine parts bought in Poland were sold on the black market in Istanbul; jeans bought in Istanbul were sold on the black market in Poland. Ercuman didn't like the Poles. They were profiteers, he said. And they were far too noisy. Several people had left the hotel because of them.

The next morning, I stayed in bed till noon. When I'm tired, I don't hesitate to loaf. More than once, I've stayed in bed all day. When you travel, you have to conserve your strength. Trudge about tired, and you wear yourself out. A mistake, that. The worst traveler is a weary traveler.

Weary, you're apt to become depressed. Which is not what you want at all. Depression must be nipped in the bud. Fail to recognize its early stages and, before you know it, it's taken the upper hand. Soon, it's out of control completely, and however much you try, your spirits just won't be revived. The only course then is to head for home.

When my spirits start to flag, I indulge myself. A small extravagance usually does the trick: a night in a good hotel, a nice dinner (a break from my usual diet of bread and cheese), a film. When the case is extreme, I will telephone home. And my family, knowing why I call—but naturally avoiding all mention of it—will tell me how much they envy me.

"The weather's been awful," they'll say. "Nothing but rain for over a week."

Or, "I thought of you on the way to work this morning. What a lucky dog you are!"

None of this is true. They hate to travel. Away from home for more than a day, they begin to lose weight. But it never fails to work, this conversation. By the time I hang up, I'm my old self again. The blues have been put to flight.

―――――

Osman was harder to find than we realized. Ercuman made his inquiries, and I made mine, but neither of us had any luck. I even recruited Selim. He didn't approve, of course, but he promised to check around. He got nowhere, either.

Everyone I talked to knew of Osman and remembered him fondly. What an old crook, they said laughing. What a rascal. More laughter. But not one of them could tell me where to find him. Osman had dropped out of sight.

"His name doesn't come up anymore," said one man. "You're the first person I've heard mention him in years."

Ercuman refused to be discouraged. He'd locate Osman eventually, he didn't doubt. But it would take a little time.

"Didn't you say you wanted to see the rest of Turkey?" he said. "Why not do that now? By the time you get back, I'll have found him for you."

Not a bad idea. I'd start in Trabzon, the leading city on the Black Sea coast.

"Take a ferry," said Ercuman. "It's more fun than going overland."

Selim was shocked when I told him my plans.

"Are you serious?" he said. "Trabzon is awful. Still, it might be endured for a day or two. You are coming right back, aren't you?"

"Well, not immediately," I said. "I want to explore a bit. After Trabzon, I'm off to Kars."

"Kars," he spluttered. "I can't believe this. Kars is a hole."

"And then I'm going to Doubayazit."

He slapped his forehead.

"And Van," I went on, enjoying the effect I was having. "And from there to Cappadocia . . . "

He covered his ears.

"Enough, enough," he pleaded. "You're crazy. You'll never get back alive."

"I won't?"

"Not a chance," he said. "You'll come to a bad end. Is that what you want?"

Well, not exactly—though I wouldn't mind a fate worthy of Walter Scott: permanent exile, madness, retreat to a monastery. And if not that, what? At the very least, I'd have an adventure or two. Among the books in my backpack were several written by earlier visitors to Turkey: David Urquhart's *Spirit of the East* (1838), Warburton's *The Crescent and the Cross* (1845), Joseph Wolff's *Travels and Adventures* (1860), and Fred Burnaby's *On Horseback Through Asia Minor* (1876). Theirs was the Turkey I was seeking. The Turkey of a century ago. Were I just to have a fraction of *their* adventures, I'd leave this country a happy man.

"Have you any idea what Anatolia is like?" Selim wanted to know.

"I think so. Mountains in the north and south, no? And a plateau in the middle."

"*High* mountains. Which you'll have to cross to get to Kars. And at this time of year, the plateau is semidesert. Hardly anyone lives there. I wish you'd reconsider."

"There are towns, aren't there?"

"If you can call them that. Miserable, poverty-stricken places. I have a book an American gave me. I want you to read it before you go anywhere."

According to Selim's book, the Anatolia plateau is never less than 2,600 feet above sea level and is not continuous. Valleys alternate with high crags, rounded hills with basins, and wide depressions with steppeland—level, treeless plains supporting little more than sheep and goats. In summer extremely hot and in winter extremely cold, the region receives little rainfall. Per capita income is the lowest in Turkey.

The book went on to quote John Dewey. The Anatolian plateau, said the American educator, "is nothing more than some of our western plateaus, modified by the foothills of the Rockies; treeless as far as the eye can reach; occasional herds of sheep and cattle; here and there grain fields which testify to a precarious 'dry farming'; almost no houses, the occasional village, small and tucked away in a ravine in the side of some hill, eroded as if to serve as a geological model for a class of students in physical geography."

"Doubayazit, Van, Cappadocia—they're all in Anatolia," said Selim. "Take my advice: stay away from it."

He was not the only one to deplore my plans. Istanbul is not like the rest of Turkey, people told me again and again. In Anatolia, that part of Turkey that lies in Asia, there would be no productions of Chekhov; no Lions Club; no Chicken McNuggets. To leave Istanbul was to leave civilization.

They made the city sound like a prodigy that, against all odds, had overcome its modest circumstances and made a mark in the world. Anatolia was the embarrassing relative: crude, vulgar, unlettered. Worse: for all of Istanbul's success, Anatolia was destined to stay that way.

"You'll be very uncomfortable," said Selim. "Do you think you're up to it?"

"Burnaby was."

Selim knew about Burnaby. I'd shown him my books.

"You're no Burnaby," he said, not unkindly.

Maybe I wasn't. Maybe no one was anymore. But that was another reason to take this trip: to get a look at the modern traveler in Turkey. What were these people like? Did they resemble at all their illustrious forebears?

Despite Selim's warnings, I didn't fear coming to grief in Anatolia. The Turks I'd met had been much too kind. Just the other day, I had gone to his office because I wanted to type a letter. He was on deadline when I got there—those topless women were about to go to press—but instead of asking me to wait, he found a typewriter for me. And then he found me a desk. And a chair. And some typing paper. He hadn't finished yet. Before returning to his pictures, he gathered up those colleagues who spoke English and sent them to talk to me.

"Take care of him," he told them.

I couldn't use the typewriter, as it happened. It had a Turkish keyboard, which is utterly unlike an American one. Selim suggested that I use the telex machine, whose keyboard is more conventional. This worked nicely until, halfway through, UPI sent a story from New York, and before I knew it, both the story and my letter were whisked to the news desk and appeared, for all I know, in the next edition.

At this point, I was ready to give up. But Selim wouldn't hear of it. He had thought of another possibility: the British Council.

"They'll have a typewriter you can use," he said. "I'll give them a call."

But the council couldn't help. Their typewriters were all in use. Another setback. But it didn't matter to Selim. He had another idea: *Dateline,* an English-language weekly published down the street.

He drew a blank there, too, but I couldn't help but admire his resourcefulness. How indefatigable he was. Who could fail to be impressed by such resilience?

This kind of solicitude is a Turkish trait. At my hotel, I

wasn't allowed to sit on the front steps in case I compromise my jeans; in the mornings, a waiter shooed away any wasps that threatened to spoil my breakfast; Ercuman moved a desk into my room to make it easier for me to work; and when I inquired once why the hotel's neon sign wasn't lighted—it isn't when the hotel is full, I learned later—I was asked if I would rather that it were.

Turks are so solicitous, one hesitates to betray any inadequacy. Even seek directions and a task force is assembled. How eager they are to help, providing advice, prices, opening hours, bus schedules. They'll do anything to be of service, anything to smooth your way.

Just as my first had been, my last night in Istanbul was disturbed by a detonation. Actually, a series of detonations. Not falling masonry this time, but gunshots. The police, armed with automatic weapons, were on the scene in seconds. Ercuman was furious when they suggested that the shots might have come from our hotel.

"We have no sympathy for Kurds," he shouted. "We do not harbor terrorists."

But the police insisted on searching the place anyway. I was rather hoping they might cart off the Poles. They had been howling more than usual of late. I hadn't slept in nearly a week.

chapter 2

My first night at sea was no improvement. The couple in the next cabin argued back and forth for hours. I didn't sleep a wink.

Actually, it was hardly an argument. It was more a monologue: the woman, shrill and indignant, enumerating a long list of complaints and dissatisfactions; the man confining himself to an occasional placatory aside.

First, she ranted because the cabin was too small. And then she raved because the porthole wouldn't open. But what really got her going was the discovery that she'd lost her sunglasses. Not her fault, this. His. Why couldn't he have thought to keep an eye on them?

"You can replace them in Trabzon," he said. Which only incensed her more.

"That's your answer to everything, isn't it?" she said. "Spend, spend, spend. And what makes you think they can be replaced? That's the trouble with you..."

And so on and so on until, tired out, she finally fell quiet.

Not so the old man with whom I was sharing a cabin. He had a problem with his breathing, not so much inhaling air as gobbling it. Now that gobbling intensified until he was gulping, gulping with such force, he sounded as if he might be choking.

I got out of bed and shook him awake.

"Are you all right?" I asked.

"Never better," he said—and went back to sleep. He gulped for the rest of the night.

I kept my sanity by imagining the meals I was going to have on board this ship. It was my plan to replicate exactly a dinner Warburton had when sailing to Alexandria in 1844: "Soup, fish, meat, poultry, confectionary, and fruit, irrigated freely by claret, hock, port and sherry."

Yes, that would certainly hit the spot. But first I'd have a very large breakfast. Plenty of fresh rolls and oodles of honey. An abundance of cheese and masses of olives. And torrents of tea. Enough tea to drown a cat.

But instead of rolls and honey, breakfast consisted of French fries and a salad.

"There's nothing else?" I asked the steward.

"There may be rice somewhere," he said. "But it's probably cold."

Lunch would be better, I consoled myself, not knowing that French fries and salad and rice were all we would be offered for the next three days.

But worse than the food was the frenzy at mealtimes. The cafeteria was small, and we were many, and the result was a noisy free-for-all. People pushed and shoved and lost their tempers. They raised their voices and said unpleasant things to one another. They rattled their sabers and threatened to come to blows. Arguments broke out—fierce arguments usually having to do with definitions of tenure. If A reached a table before B did, was it rightfully A's if B had seen it first? Or, could B occupy a seat vacated by A if A had left it intending to return?

The Turkish love of complication added a further wrinkle. In order to eat, one had first to buy from the purser coupons, which one then tendered, in lieu of money, in exchange for food. It was more a nuisance than anything, but for some reason people never got the hang of it, and there were endless delays while the cashier said he couldn't take francs or marks or guilders; and people demanded to know what he had against these currencies; and he said he had nothing against them; and they said, then why wouldn't he take them? and he said he wasn't allowed to; and they said they'd never heard anything so ridiculous, adding for effect that in Paris or Bonn or Amsterdam, they did things differently. By which they meant, of course, that they did things better.

It was bedlam. Sheer bedlam.

And then there was the discomfort of eating with strangers. At breakfast that first morning, a couple sat themselves at my table and proceeded to monopolize it. First, they put their books on it, and after that their cameras. And then they pushed both books and cameras to my side of the table, in order that they might play cards. That's when they started to argue, and I recognized them as the couple in the cabin next to mine, the couple who had kept me up all night.

Paying me no heed, the woman upbraided her companion because she hadn't been able to take a bath, because her morning tea had failed to arrive, and because the ship was full. This last rankled most. Had she known that so many others were going to Trabzon, she said, she would have gone somewhere else.

A small woman in her early fifties, she had a face that was all sharp points: her nose, her chin, even her ears, which her tightly cropped hair revealed to resemble those of a certain crewman on the starship *Enterprise*. When she spoke, she would throw her head back and lower it again, over and over like a pelican easing a fish into its gullet.

"You know I hate crowds," she said accusingly.

Her husband offered nothing in reply. A man as shapeless

as a beanbag, he sat there gazing at his hands, his round, neutral, no-man's-land of a face empty of expression. This was self-effacement at its most craven. Or was it? He looked up at one point and, for a brief moment, I thought I saw anger in his eyes. And then he returned to examining his hands. Big hands. Big enough to strangle someone. Was it possible that this meek-looking man had murder in his heart?

I felt suddenly sick—the French fries, no doubt—and I prayed to God we wouldn't hit rough seas. The Black Sea is notoriously unpredictable. I took a turn around the deck in the hope it would calm my stomach.

I liked this boat. Nominally a ferry, it was handsome enough to be a cruise ship. Painted white, it had three decks and a flat stern, through which cars were loaded. This morning, we were being escorted by a flotilla of sea gulls. There were far too many. And what a racket they made. Nag, nag, nag. There was something menacing about these birds. Wheeling about in that belligerent way of theirs, they brought to mind the woman who had lost her sunglasses.

It was still early, and the only other person on deck was the man with whom I was sharing a cabin. A Turk, he was almost blind and had trouble walking. The latter difficulty, from what I could gather, had something to do with arthritis. Everything he did required huge effort. Simply getting out of bed this morning had taken almost five minutes.

First, he had to pull himself into a sitting position, and then he waited until his breathing eased. He was ready now to lower his legs to the floor. First one—very, very slowly—and then the other. His face racked with pain, he paused again before gripping both sides of the bunk and hauling himself to his feet.

"Can I help?" I said.

But he shook his head.

"This is God's will," he said.

A haze made it difficult to see much. Along the coast, I was able to make out a series of hills receding in ranks: black in front, then brown, blue, and bringing up the rear, gray. I did wish the light would improve. I wished, too, it were a little warmer. For the first time in two months, I was cold. I hadn't imagined Turkey being chilly. "Chilly" doesn't figure in the vocabulary of flight. It wasn't to the frigid north I dreamed of escaping, but to the torrid south. But this was far from torrid, and I was just a little disappointed. I went below and put on socks. The first socks I'd worn since getting here.

Back on deck, the first person I saw was the woman who'd spoiled my breakfast. She was feeding water biscuits to a poodle. Her companion was nowhere in sight. No doubt, he was catching up on his sleep. She saw me look around for somewhere to sit and signaled to the chair beside her.

"I'm Valerie Locke," she said, extending a hand that still contained a water biscuit. "From Manchester. I hope we didn't embarrass you in the cafeteria. My husband and I argue all the time. I call us the Clashing Lockes."

She pointed to the book lying open on her lap: *Jason and the Argonauts.*

"You know. Like the clashing rocks. We saw them last night when we entered the Black Sea. They were said to crush anything that passed between them. Until Jason came along. After that, the clashing rocks clashed no more."

She laughed.

"Not us, though. We just go on fighting. It relieves the monotony."

"I don't think monotony should be relieved," I said. I still hadn't forgiven her for keeping me awake. "It should be ended."

"And how does one do that?"

"Change the conditions that cause it."

She laughed again.

"How little you know about the world," she said. "You have to be younger than you look."

Argumentative to a fault, she took issue with almost everything I said. She asked if I liked boats, and I said I did. She didn't. And said so at length. She asked if I liked Istanbul. I said I did. She didn't. And again said so at length. I liked Turkish food, and she didn't; Turkish music, and she didn't; Turkish wine, and she didn't.

It was very exhausting, and I was actually excusing myself when I was cut short by a startled shout. It issued from my cabin mate. A waiter had brought him a pastry, and he had just begun to eat when a sea gull, bigger and more daring than the others, swooped down with a fearful cawing and snatched it from his hand.

We looked up in time to see the bird begin its ascent, but as it did so, the pastry fell from its grasp. Furious now, the gull swooped again, its target this time the old man himself. With its beak, it stabbed him on the head—stabbed him hard—and seemed about to strike again when it was driven off, complaining mightily, by a steward flapping a tablecloth.

It was awful, the more so because the victim had been so vulnerable. Another person might have run away. This man couldn't. Another person might have defended himself. He couldn't do that, either. Almost blind, he couldn't *see* his attacker, much less ward him off. Almost blind, he couldn't know if his assailant was one or many. He must have been terrified.

"My God!" said Mrs. Locke as the stewards took him to his cabin. "It's right out of *Jason and the Argonauts*. Don't you see? Phineus, the blind king, being attacked by the Harpies. This is exquisite."

"Not exquisite for him," I said. "It scared him half to death."

"Of course, it didn't," she said. "Anyway, why is a blind man traveling alone? Doesn't he have relatives? Really, people are just *too* thoughtless."

Watched by the poodle, his wet nose quivering with interest, she resumed her reading. I liked this dog, and so did most of those on board. He had many more friends than Mrs. Locke did. When the two of them came on deck, it was to him that people talked, not to her.

"Are you well?" they would ask, patting his head. "Not seasick, are we?"

And then they would move on, not having said a word to his dyspeptic owner.

Not that she seemed to mind. I think she loved that dog and was pleased to see him get attention. Certainly, she treated him better than she did her husband. She didn't ever raise her voice to him. And when she read, she would glance at the dog before she turned a page, as if to be sure she had his permission. Her relationship with this animal was anthropomorphic to a fault.

Mrs. Locke sighed and closed her book.

"I've been thinking about that sea gull," she said. "It's an omen. Something very unpleasant—"

She broke off.

"What does that man think he's doing?"

A young German sitting near us had wedged his knee between his girlfriend's thighs and was fondling her breast.

"Really," said Mrs. Locke. "Those Germans are shameless."

Just last night, she said, she had seen two of them coupling behind a lifeboat.

"They're like the Mossynoeci. You haven't heard of the Mossynoeci? That's because you haven't read *Jason and the Argonauts*."

48

She started to thumb through her book.

"Here we are," she said, and started to read aloud: " 'The Mossynoeci have their own ideas of what is right and proper. What we as a rule do openly in town or market-place they do at home; and what we do in the privacy of our houses they do out of doors in the open street, and nobody thinks the worse of them. Even the sexual act puts no one to the blush in this community. On the contrary, like swine in the fields, they lie down on the ground in promiscuous intercourse and are not at all disconcerted by the presence of others.' "

She put the book down.

"Isn't it amazing?" she said. "First Phineus, and now the Mossynoeci. Everyone in the *Argonautica* is represented on this ship. See the man on the bridge? That's Ancaeus, the helmsman. And the boy with the guitar? Orpheus the musician."

"And who do you represent?" I said.

"Medea, of course. Medea could 'arrest a star and check the movement of the sacred moon.' She was a sorceress."

"You work spells?"

"Naturally. Why do you think my husband puts up with me? He's bewitched."

"Which of the Argonauts am I?" I said.

"I don't know you well enough to say. What are you doing in Turkey?"

Since she was being unusually nice, I told her about my search for Osman.

"But that's perfect," she said, quite delighted. "Don't you see? Osman is your golden fleece. That makes you Jason."

"I can't be," I said. "There's nothing heroic about me."

"There was nothing heroic about Jason, either. He was a callow youth. A mere boy. A bungler."

That afternoon, we made a stop in Sinop. Traders were setting up shop on the wharf when we entered the harbor and were hawking their wares long before the ship docked. They wore plastic bags on their heads to protect them from a light rain. One beat a ladle on a pot filled with cooking corn. The police watched us as we disembarked. Why were they here? Was it to ensure our safety? Or were they looking for someone?

Today, the traders did little business. People stocked up on cigarettes and replenished their supplies of fruit, but there was call for little else. No one wanted corn on the cob or shish kebabs or ice cream, any more than coffee or tea or bottled water. You would think that, after the dreadful fare of the past two days, we would have fallen on these things. But the truth was that none of us could any longer *think* of eating. Because of those French fries and all that rice, the mere thought of food was enough to turn our stomachs.

The traders—they were Turks, after all—took this in their stride. It was always much like this, one of them told me. They arranged their wares; the ship docked; the passengers browsed briefly; the ship left. And the traders, after watching it go, pushed their barrows back to town.

And yet they continued to come here. Week in, week out, the boat put in, and there they were. Why did they bother? Was it habit? The absence of something better to do? Or did they believe that, one day, passengers would descend from this ship like ravening hordes and buy everything in sight? I did hope it was the latter. Faith is enormously appealing.

Built on a wide bay and surrounded by cornfields that come down to the water, Sinop—what little I saw of it—discouraged closer inspection. There were cranes and a warehouse and a petroleum store and racks of tobacco leaves curing in the sun. The houses behind the port looked battered.

"Sinop was leveled by the Russians in eighteen fifty-three," the purser told us, making us wish that we'd gotten here sooner. A planned bus tour was quietly canceled.

Soon, we were on our way once more, but not for long. Two hours out, misfortune struck: one of our engines failed.

"We'll never get to Trabzon on just one engine," said the barman. "The Black Sea is much too treacherous."

Indeed, it has a reputation for meanness. The Pacific is known for being mighty, and the Atlantic for being fierce. The Black Sea has made a name for itself by being querulous. It can turn nasty in a moment, storms springing up from nowhere and with little warning.

The other engine was shut down while the first was being repaired. This meant that we were now without stabilizers, and we floundered in a rough sea while work proceeded. The crew toiled mightily, but progress was slow. An hour passed. And then a second. And then a third. The ship was rolling more than ever now, groaning like the *Argo*'s speaking beam, and little by little, the deck emptied. Passengers were returning to their cabins, slipping away, offering the excuse that they were feeling queasy. They needed privacy, they said. They didn't care to be sick in public.

Mrs. Locke, after her initial satisfaction that her prediction had proved accurate, turned green.

"I'm going to die," she moaned. And then, as was her wont, she turned on her husband.

"Well, don't just stand there," she howled. "Do something."

"Do what?" he pleaded.

"Borrow a gun from someone. Throw me overboard. End this misery."

Her discomfort reminded me of the unhappy Turkish woman

whose mal de mer had so amused Fred Burnaby. "In despairing tones, she called for assistance," he wrote in 1876. Her "black attendant rushed to the rescue and convulsively grasped the lady's head. It was a funny spectacle—that enormous pumpkin-shaped face supported by two black hands." Funny? I hardly think so. Is it possible that Burnaby was callous?

Mr. Locke bore his stricken spouse downstairs. I chose to stay in the lounge. I was feeling ill myself, but I was determined to fight it. Perhaps if I were occupied. . . . I applied myself with great assiduity to the adventures of Joseph Wolff. The good doctor had crossed the Black Sea several times. And usually in bad weather. Yet he never once was sick. He had a formula. To avoid becoming ill, he said, you didn't wear a hat; you slept on the floor; and first thing every morning, you doused yourself with seawater.

I resolved to begin this regimen the very next day. But that wouldn't help me now. My head was pounding, and my palms were sweating. And then, for good measure, the soles of my feet began to tingle.

The barman said something I couldn't hear.

"What's that?"

"I said, 'Are you all right?' "

His voice sounded unusually distant.

"I think so," I said. "Why?"

"You've turned an odd shade of yellow."

If only the wretched floor wouldn't heave so! It was fairly pitching around now, chairs and tables—those that weren't screwed down—scudding from one end of the lounge to the other.

"Do you think they'll be much longer?" I asked the barman. But I didn't hear his answer. My stomach gave a lurch. And then it lurched again. This was a stomach on the move. It meant to relocate.

"You'll have to excuse me," I said, struggling to my feet. "I think I should lie down."

I lay on my bunk and prayed for sleep. And when that didn't work—the bloody Lockes chose just then to have another argument—I prayed for death. Why is it, that when you really need oblivion, you can never find it?

The argument next door continued, Mrs. Locke apparently blaming her husband for the failure of the engine. It was something he might have anticipated, she said; any normal person booking passage on a ship would have insisted on seeing the engine room.

Then, to make matters worse, a storm struck. At the mercy of the elements now, the ship creaked and quivered. Giant waves thundered against the hull, and a driving rain lashed the deck. The sky had grown quite dark. We were surrounded on all sides by an impenetrable murk.

The wind shrieked. But loud as it shrieked, Mrs. Locke shrieked louder. She shrieked so loud that even her husband became alarmed and appealed to me for help.

"She's a bit hysterical," he said. "I wonder if you'd have a word with her. She won't listen to me."

But Mrs. Locke was not in a mood to listen to anyone.

"We're going to go down," she said. And then she sat bolt upright. "Did you hear that?" Her eyes were wide with terror. "That was a cracking sound. The ship is breaking up. We're going to drown."

Her husband looked at me pleadingly. I was expected to offer solace, something I'm not very good at. I become deranged when people get upset. I never say the right thing.

I patted Mrs. Locke on the hand.

"Oh, drowning's not so bad," I said, trying to sound jolly. "I almost drowned myself once, and believe me, I've never been so unmoved by anything. All that stuff about mortal dread and quaking with fear? Nonsense, all of it. Drowning is boring."

Mrs. Locke gazed at me as if she couldn't believe her ears. Still, she had stopped howling. Drawing encouragement from that, I pressed on.

"But for some reason"—and here I laughed lightly—"my parents could never be convinced of this, and for years afterwards the word *water* was banished from the family lexicon. No mention of water or water biscuits or watercolors or water beds. But that was just the start of it. In time, the ban was extended to anything *connoting* water: beaches, fish, irrigation, shampoo, umbrellas, dehydrated milk, tear ducts, mouth-to-mouth resuscitation."

I was babbling—making no sense at all—and I knew it. Mr. Locke knew it, too. He was looking frantic, signaling me to stop. But I couldn't. I had been seized by madness.

"I remember a friend of my father's coming to dinner one evening," I resumed, "and he mentioned Jacques Cousteau. One casual reference. That's all. But that was enough for my mother. He was never asked to the house again. A strange woman, my mother. I once saw her drown a cat. I was very young—no more than two or three—but I've never forgotten the noise it made."

Mrs. Locke had grabbed feebly for her husband's hand and was struggling to say something. She looked utterly drained.

"Get him out of here," she said in a whisper. "Get him out before he kills me."

Just then, as suddenly as it had started, the storm stopped. Where, a moment before, there had been just fury, all now was placid. No crashing waves, no driving rain, no howling wind. Just a deep calm. The sky lightened, the murk dispersed, and the sun came out. Stretching before us was the open sea.

"We are saved," said Mrs. Locke, her panic subsiding. "We have come through hell alive."

And uttering a loud moan, she fainted on her husband's neck.

Later that evening, the ship now restored to full power, I came upon them in the bar. She was lying, Pietàlike, in his arms and, in piteous tones, was telling him how frightened she had been. For his part, he gazed into that stricken face with such tenderness, it brought a lump to my throat. I do believe he loved her very much.

I went on deck and watched a seaman take down the Turkish flag. He did so with little ceremony. No sounding of taps, no standing at attention, no rifles fired in salute. The national colors were bundled up as if they were a piece of washing. I had heard that Turks love their flag. Love it with a passion. It was a reminder to me to be skeptical of what one hears. Much of it is nonsense.

Most of the Europeans having gone to bed, the deck began to fill with Turks. This was their favorite time of day: for an hour or two, they had the place to themselves. While they were never less than kind, I think they found us something of a puzzle. We were so unlike them, after all. Noisy and strident and much too self-assertive. And our men and women—the easy way they mingled. How it had to astonish them!

On deck this evening were two brothers in their late teens. For the past two days, the younger of the two had been keeping company with a man from Oslo. The Norwegian was obviously homosexual, but the boy's parents seemed not to mind. When they saw them together, they would nod and smile.

"Why don't they do something?" Mrs. Locke had asked the barman.

"Why would they?" he said. "They're Greek."

Actually, they weren't, but since Turks hold Greeks in very low esteem, it was all the explanation he needed.

The Lockes were unusually quiet that night—no doubt because Mrs. Locke was indisposed—and I managed to get some sleep. The next morning, though, saw her back in form, and I was wakened shortly after daybreak by what I can best describe as her liveliest performance yet. Apparently, her tea had failed to appear again.

These exchanges were taking their toll on Mr. Locke, and increasingly I would find him in the bar, staring into a glass of beer. It was in just such an attitude that I found him after breakfast.

"How is your wife?" I asked.

"Acting up a little, I'm afraid," he said. "No doubt, you heard."

"Getting you down, is it?"

"A bit. Still, there's not much I can do about it. Is there?"

"Oh, I don't know. You could try telling her to stop. Be firm with her."

"Firm?" he said, as though the idea surprised him. "With Valerie, you mean?"

"Why not?"

"Oh, I couldn't do that. It's her nerves, you see. She'd be fine if it weren't for her nerves."

The mist had cleared, making it possible to see the coast again. It was lovely—a stretch of turquoise water and, behind it, lots of rearing mountains, many of them wooded. The peaks closest to the sea were dotted with tiny white houses surrounded by yellow meadows. Soon, we were passing a bright green headland. And then we came in sight of a good-sized town girdling an attractive harbor. In the distance was a bank of blue-black clouds. It looked as if it might be raining.

An hour later, the mist returned, and we slipped into a torpor. Life afloat had become routine. It had ceased to surprise—which is the same as saying it had begun to disappoint. Spend too much time at sea, and you begin to fancy yourself a lost soul. Somewhere on the other side of that mist, there existed a real world—a solid world. Not an ever-changing world like this. How we longed to be part of it. Longed as mightily as Chekhov's Olga longed for Moscow. And the more we longed, the more like a purgatory the ship became. This was a half life, something to be suffered until we made that happy shore and took our places among God's elect.

Typically, Mrs. Locke longed more loudly than anyone.

"How many are there on this boat?" she asked.

"I'm guessing," I said. "Three hundred? Four hundred?"

"And how many hotel rooms are there in Trabzon?"

"I have no idea. Why?"

"I don't think it has very many. You know what that means, don't you? Some of these people will end up sleeping in the street."

If they did, I didn't see the Pullman crowd minding very much. That was Mrs. Locke's name for the Mossynoeci—the young Germans who eschewed cabins and slept in the lounge in Pullman chairs. There were more than a hundred of them, and Mrs. Locke loved to belittle them.

"Why must they behave as if no one existed but themselves?" she wanted to know.

For my part, I rather liked them.

They didn't venture into the cafeteria. They didn't need to. Self-sufficient, they had brought their own provisions: cucumbers and peaches, bread and sardines, salami and boiled eggs, cheese and pâté—all of which they ate from the blades of penknives. I found myself avoiding their mealtimes. Too awful to imagine those blades slicing through their tender tongues.

They were not the tidiest of people, these Germans. After a repast, they left behind them tables strewn with carrot shavings and orange peels, empty cans and bread crusts, milk cartons and cheese rinds. But I admired them, anyway. Not least for the equipment they had to carry: bulging backpacks, and tents, and sleeping bags, and cooking equipment, and fishing rods, and hunting knives, and books, and radios, and much, much more. I have never seen people more encumbered. Loading up, they would wobble under all that weight; loading down, they would drop to their knees like camels.

The Pullman crowd cared little for the soft vicissitudes of comfort and repose. They had come to Turkey to experience nature. And while I wished them luck, I was glad I wasn't one of them. Where discomfort was concerned, I preferred the urban kind. I didn't mind being mugged or being murdered in my sleep. I didn't mind heart failure brought about by hypertension or hearing loss brought on by too much noise. I didn't mind streets gangs or stray bullets or even serial killers. What I did mind—a lot—was sleeping in the great outdoors.

"What? You don't want to sleep beneath the stars?" said a Pullman person—a man whose plan it was to ride a motorbike to India.

Not without an intervening roof, I don't. But it isn't the stars I fear, it's what we call "the wild." In the wild, too much can go wrong. People are bitten by snakes in the wild. They are swept away by flash floods. Trees fall on them. They lose their way and starve to death. They're nudged awake at night by slavering beasts feasting on their feet. Not my cup of tea at all.

I wish I could be more attached to nature. I quite like it, of course. But to embrace it completely, I'd have to trust it more. And truth to tell, I don't trust it at all. It's too unpredictable. I do with nature what I do with people whose moods are unreliable. As much as I can, I steer clear of them.

The chap going to India wore leather trousers and a leather jacket. His hair needed washing, and his face was as white as powdered sugar. He looked like Edward Scissorhands. When we docked in Giresun that afternoon, he and I went looking for a teahouse.

"Look, there's one over there," he said, as we left the harbor.

It was small and cluttered and full of men whose lassitude suggested a life of unemployment. We sat at a small wooden table and ordered bottled water. A picture of Ataturk was partially obscured by steam rising from a tea urn. A cat brushed against my leg. A fly settled on my forehead.

The water had still to arrive when two of our shipmates walked in: the man from Oslo and his young companion. The latter addressed a question to the man making tea—a brutish looking fellow who seemed less than pleased to see him. His answer—though I didn't catch it—was obviously dismissive. The boy spoke again, and this time the tea maker, by way of reply, waved him away with his hand. He wanted him to leave.

"What's all that about?" I asked the man in leather.

"I think he said he won't serve Greeks."

"But he *isn't* Greek."

"I don't think it matters. He doesn't like him."

"Because he's gay?"

"Maybe."

All eyes were on the boy now. The tea drinkers put down their glasses, and the smokers laid aside their pipes. The cat darted under a table. The murmur of conversation ceased. But for the buzzing of the flies, the place was silent.

"We should go," said the Norwegian.

But the boy didn't move.

"Out," said the tea man.

The boy glanced around him. He had begun to look irresolute. But still he stood his ground.

Turning a bright red, the tea man rose to his feet and lumbered to the center of the room. He was bigger than I thought him. My chair shook when he passed it. He kicked over several tables and then took off his jacket.

"Oh-oh," said the German. "He wants to fight."

"He mustn't," I said. "He'll kill him."

The Norwegian grabbed the boy's arm.

"It's time we left," he said.

But the boy pulled himself free and went to meet his challenger. The two belligerents squared off, circling each other, weaving their bodies, their fists raised to shield their faces. And then the tea man made his move, lunging at the hapless boy with such force that I shut my eyes.

It's over, I thought.

I heard a thud and then a moan. It was followed a moment later by a gasp of surprise and the sound of something hitting the floor. Hitting it hard.

I opened my eyes, expecting the teenager to be flat on his back. And someone *was* down. But it wasn't the boy. The boy was on his feet. It was the tea man, wearing a look of dazed astonishment, who lay sprawled. A table—knocked over when he hit the deck—had fallen across his chest.

The man in leather was jubilant when we walked back to the ship.

"What happened exactly?" I said. "I stopped looking when the big one pounced. I thought that was it."

"It would have been if the kid hadn't jumped out of his way. Man, was he quick! And then, before the other could recover, he wheeled around and kicked him on the side of the head. It was beautiful!"

"He *kicked* him?"

He laughed and slapped his leather thigh.

"Isn't that wild? He's a kick boxer. That's what he does for a living. And no one had any idea."

I realized later that it might have been the Amycus incident in the Jason story: the Argonauts meeting up with nasty King

Amycus; the brutish monarch challenging Pollux to a fight, not knowing that Pollux, though a mere boy, was already a boxing champion; Pollux felling Amycus; brain winning another victory over brawn.

Needless to say, I mentioned none of this to Mrs. Locke. That woman was credulous enough as it was. The last thing she needed was encouragement.

chapter 3

I fled that ferry the moment it docked in Trabzon. It was my intention to beat my shipmates to the hotels. But the plan misfired. Seeing me take off—and mistaking my flight for purpose—they assumed I was familiar with Trabzon and promptly gave chase. When I glanced behind me, there they were—forty or fifty of them in hot pursuit. As Joseph Conrad's Kurtz would say, "The horror!"

Finding the hotels would have been easy had I just known where they were. But first I had to look for them. And this proved something of a problem. A search of the harbor yielded nothing— just mounds of moldering cargo dotted about like haystacks in an autumn field. Trabzon proper occupied the hill above me, but I couldn't seem to get there. Every time I turned inland, I was met sooner or later by a wall of rock.

My pursuers were undeterred by any of this. There was simply no shaking them. They slowed when I slowed, turned when I turned, stopped when I stopped. When I looked about me, they looked about them; my glancing up was *their* signal to glance up; and once, when I dashed across a street, they dashed, too, bringing Trabzon's traffic to a screeching halt.

It should have been clear to them that I had no idea where

I was going. But no. They saw my constantly changing course as an effort to cover my tracks. The more lost I became, the more assiduously they followed me, certain now I knew something they didn't, sure that I was going to extraordinary lengths to keep it to myself.

They were still hot on my heels when, dodging behind a newsstand, I spotted a dark, narrow street winding its way uphill. Strange I wouldn't have seen it sooner. I had been past this newsstand twice before. Had I simply missed it? Or was this sorcery? Trabzon had once been famous for its necromancy. Had some magic summoned this street into being?

I made my way upwards and found myself in a large plaza—a cobbled square of shops and restaurants and a huge tea garden ablaze with flowers. My pursuers exchanged looks of triumph. So this was my little secret. This was why I had tried to elude them.

It was apparent right away that Trabzon is no ordinary place. Though it was fast approaching sunset—a time when flags are normally lowered—in Trabzon, a flag had just been *raised*. But more curious still was the fact that no one here was moving. The national anthem blared from a loudspeaker, and everyone in the plaza stood frozen at attention. Even the shoeblacks had interrupted their labors—as indicative as anything of the great love the Turk has for his country.

For a moment, I let myself pretend that Trabzon had been enchanted. It had incurred the wrath of a vengeful genie, and this was the price it had to pay—to remain like this, frozen in time, until the genie relented and life could be resumed.

It did not resume for quite some time. National anthems are invariably long and dreary, and Turks, not to be outdone, have taken as theirs an anthem as long and dreary as any in existence. I could have left, I suppose, but I didn't care to give offense. Was

I being fastidious? Certainly my shipmates thought so. Unlike me, they had bolted and were even now filling to capacity what few hotel rooms Trabzon had to offer.

There was one more surprise when the playing stopped, and the people around me began to speak. They spoke not in Turkish, but in English. And not just standard English. This was English spoken with an Irish accent. Now I was utterly convinced. Trabzon *was* enchanted.

Not quite, it turned out. These people were soccer fans here for a tournament that would last all week. I had picked the worst possible time to visit Trabzon. Every hotel in town was full to overflowing.

I ended up joining forces with the man in leather. He and his wife had found a modest room, which they offered to let me share. They were acting, they said, "out of consideration." Since I was paying for my *one* bed as much as they were paying for their *two*, the arrangement was more considerate of them than it was of me. But I didn't complain. The alternative, I reminded myself, was spending the night alfresco.

The room had a concrete floor, blue walls, a low ceiling, one naked light bulb, and three wooden beds.

"My bed wobbles," said the man in leather.

"My bed sags," said his wife.

"My bed doesn't have a pillow," said I.

"There's a hole in the wall," said the man in leather.

"The sink is broken," said his wife.

"The door won't shut," said I.

"Terrible place," said the man in leather. "I expected more for three dollars a night."

"It's awful," his wife agreed. "I'm very disappointed."

I was, too. This place was far too comfortable. Adventure was what I wanted, and adventure meant hardship. It meant privation. It meant accommodations that turned the stomach. Like the rooms Burnaby stayed in—one reeking of urine, another shared with cows and horses and pigeons, a third dirtier than "the pig styes in many of our Leicestershire farms."

That's what I wanted. Very hard beds and very short commons. Something to test the resolve. A chance to show my mettle.

"We may find something better tomorrow," said the man in leather.

"Let's hope so," I said.

In the meantime, I could sleep on the floor. It would toughen me up.

The Germans looked so alike they would have passed for brother and sister. Besides dressing the same—they wore identical leather suits—they had similar Roman noses and similar double chins. They were pale and overweight and gorged themselves on biscuits. They often complained of being tired. I think they can't have been too healthy.

I left to have a spot of dinner and found the plaza jammed with people. The local soccer club had taken on Bray Wanderers—a team from Ireland—and Trabzon had emerged the victor. There was much rejoicing. But not the boisterous kind with which fans in Europe celebrate their triumphs. There were no cheering mobs overturning buses, no youngsters drunk with joy smashing shop windows and setting fire to cars.

There was nothing like that at all. No hurled bottles, no shouted obscenities, no vomiting on other people's shoes. On the evidence, I would have to say that Turks have much to learn about such things. Really! Grins and high spirits were hardly good enough. Watching these people and their failure to be raucous, it struck me yet again that Turks, though they claim to have modernized this country, have a long, long way to go.

The Germans looked cast down when I got back. They had

been to see the Iranian consul, and the news was bad. They would not be allowed to enter Iran. The problem was their motorcycle. The mullahs didn't like motorbikes, the consul explained, there being no mention of Muhammad ever having ridden one.

To reach India, they would have to try another tack. But which one? Would they bypass Iran altogether and drive through Syria? (Iraq was not considered. It had recently invaded Kuwait and was in imminent danger of being invaded itself.) Or would they forget the bike and *fly* to India? Or would they ship the bike and travel to India by bus? Or would they drive to the Iranian border and take their chances? It was just possible that a sympathetic official might agree to let them through.

They had any number of options, and each they discussed compulsively. It was the first thing they did on waking, and the last thing they did before they fell asleep. But for all their agonizing, they never reached a decision. Not a *real* decision.

"Good," one of them would say, "that's decided then. We'll leave for the border tomorrow."

"I think that's best," the other would answer. "What's there to lose?"

But five minutes later, one or the other of them would begin to look concerned.

"You know something?" he or she would say. "It'll take three days to reach the border. If we're turned back, all that time will be wasted."

And the issue would be joined anew.

The next morning, we decided to see Trabzon together. First, though, they had to take their bike to a garage. But the bike had other ideas. It had spent the night in the hotel's courtyard, and now it wouldn't leave, becoming stuck in the narrow doorway leading to the street.

Turks relish this kind of problem, and in no time, a crowd

had gathered: twenty men with twenty ways to free this bike and send it on its way. It should be taken out backwards, one man said. No, said another, it would have to be stood on end. Someone else suggested removing the mirrors. Which was done. And when that didn't help, we removed the footrests. That didn't help, either, so the large tool chest over the back wheel was taken off. And then something else was removed. And something else and something else . . .

It was only when the mudguards were unscrewed that the bike, now virtually dismantled and hardly a bike at all, was eased, finally, into the street.

"I don't understand it," said the leather lady. "We got it through this door last night."

"Not *this* door," said a man pointing across the courtyard. "You got it through *that* door."

And there it was, another doorway a little wider than the one we stood in, but so like it that we had taken them to be the same.

The leather lady was livid that no one had bothered to mention this. For my part, I thought it rather nice. To point out our mistake risked embarrassing us. Besides, it was our motorbike, and if we wanted to take it through a door that was too small for it, then no doubt we had our reasons. Turks, it is helpful to remember, consider us rather strange, and nothing we do surprises them anymore.

Trabzon was charming—a word that would have galled the emperors who once ruled here. But that was centuries ago. When Trabzon was Trebizond, and Trebizond was grand.

Few names evoke more romance than Trebizond. (Timbuktu comes close, I suppose. And Samarkand. But I can think of no others.) A great trading post and a major seat of learning, Trebizond was famed for the luxury of its court and the splendor of its buildings. It was famous, too, for magic. Soothsayers abounded, and astrologers, and alchemists.

In Trebizond, stones and plants were said to have special powers. Employ the proper rites, and they could make one well, or they could make one sick; they could ensure success or guarantee failure. They could make the potent sterile or the sterile potent. They could revive a dwindling marriage. They could confer all sorts of things: wisdom and insight, courage and youth. They could produce altered states of consciousness. They could show one the face of God.

Trebizond's grandeur is gone now. Trabzon, today, looks shabby. The wooden mansions had walls that bulged and balconies that sagged. The stone villas had either crumbled or begun to sink. Even the apartment houses—made of concrete and relatively new—looked strangely stricken. Doors hung by a single hinge, and gutters were eaten by rust. Everything here might have been built by Adam's grandfather.

And yet Trabzon seemed splendidly indifferent to it all. Basking on that hillside with the sea curled about its feet, it reminded one of those former kings who used to fill the Pera Palas Hotel in Istanbul: old now and much reduced—but really not minding very much. Though the hour of their preeminence was gone, they didn't mourn its passing. It was nice being great, but once great was all right, too. It was much less arduous. And a lot more secure.

We walked to the citadel and palace the Byzantines had built. A long, uphill slog it was, past red-roofed houses and gardens filled with snapdragons. Past cornfields, too, and cypress stands and orange groves. Glancing back at the coast, I saw heavily wooded mountains that came right down to the sea.

We stopped more than once to catch our breath. And each time we did, people would run indoors and fetch us chairs.

"Sit down," they'd say. "It's much too hot. You need to rest."

While much depleted, the citadel was still impressive, still very much a presence. Inside were cottages and gardens and fig trees and many, many goats. Brambles covered the ancient walls—those parts that still were standing. Those parts that had collapsed had been recycled—used by the poor as building materials, transformed now into humble houses.

One didn't mind this rack and ruin. Down below us, another ancient wall had been reconstructed and had been made to look bogus. Better to leave such things alone. A ruin is a ruin, after all, and that's its special charm. However dilapidated it may be, a ruin can always claim to be authentic.

From this citadel in 1461, the emperor had watched while his city burned. The sultan's ships filled his harbor, and the sultan's armies stormed his walls. Trebizond capitulated, and the last Byzantine empire was no more. Later, the sultan toured Trebizond, ascending "to the citadel and the palace, and saw and admired the security of the one and the splendor of the other, and in every way he judged the city worthy of note."

It was all very sad, this *sic transit gloria*. Still, I don't suppose that Trebizond should be mourned *too* much. The emperor was a despot, after all. Like the sultan who succeeded him. One as bad as the other. A society in which one man may dispose of others any way he pleases is not one I'd care to live in.

"Trabzon looks so clean," said the leather lady, sounding none too happy. As a concession to the heat, she had taken off her jacket. "I thought it would be dirty."

So had I. Eastern cities were supposed to be dirty, horrendously so. Eastern cities were supposed to be squalid. "The barbarous habit of leaving the bodies of horses, camels and other beasts to rot in the streets prevails in most parts of Turkey," Henry Layard wrote in 1839.

He wasn't the first to fault Turkish sanitation, and he

wouldn't be the last. In 1876, Burnaby visited Kars—and didn't linger. "The whole sewerage of the population has been thrown in front of the buildings," he said. "A very disagreeable smell could be perceived as our horses stirred up the refuse beneath their hoofs."

More recently—in 1985—Joseph Brodsky complained that the streets of Istanbul were filthy, "piled up with refuse, which is constantly rummaged through by ravenous local cats."

I saw no rotting carcasses in Trabzon, no sewage in the streets, no piles of refuse. And while there were many cats, not one of them looked hungry, much less ravenous. Frankly, I was none too pleased. Others might applaud the absence of such things, seeing it as proof of Turkey's progress. But I missed them. Dirt lends character to a place. Clean cities are all alike. It's the sordid ones that stay in the memory.

"Shall I tell you something else I miss?" said the leather lady. "The smell of urine. Turks don't seem to piss in public."

"They piss in public toilets," said the leather man.

"I don't mean public toilets. I mean outside. In bushes, in doorways. In all the time you've been here, have you ever seen anyone piss against a wall?"

I mentioned that I'd once seen a man repair behind a tree to piss. Though nothing came of it. Perhaps he suffered a *crise de nerfs*. Islam regards the human form with horror, and even in public restrooms, men avert their bodies to avoid revealing too much of themselves. Had Muhammad had his way, he'd have banned pissing altogether.

The leather lady was staring at me.

"Are you telling me that you stood there and *watched*?"

It was true. I had. And afterwards, it gave me pause. Ordinarily, a man voiding his bladder—indoors or out—would not concern me. But when you travel, nothing, I regret to say, is beneath your interest. Every act, however small, however innocent it seems, has the potential to explain, to illuminate. One small gesture and suddenly—or this is what one hopes—the underlying pattern, the grand design, is laid bare. It adds up now. Finally, you tell yourself, it all makes sense.

Of course, epiphanies like this are few and far between. As often as not, you have to grope for the sense in things. But that only makes you more determined. The revealing detail is out there somewhere, and you have to find it. *Must* find it. So you look even when you know you shouldn't. The privacy of others is nothing to a man in search of meaning.

That night, I was sleeping on the floor again when a large animal—I can't be more precise—broke into the room and began to gorge on the biscuits the leather lady had left by her bed. It was her practice to retire with a packet of biscuits, she explained. That way if she couldn't sleep, she had something on which to snack.

Although I was too frightened to do more than glance at this animal, I knew right away what it was. It was a rat. It had to be. It had come through the hole in the wall. Or under the door, which stopped a good two inches above the threshold.

Everything about rats terrifies me. Their cunning. Their destructiveness. Their piping cries. Their numbers. (There are over six billion of them.) Their fecundity. (Pliny believed they could procreate just by licking each other.) And their appetites. Rats eat everything. Infants. Even their own young.

But more than anything, I am frightened of their teeth. Those teeth can gnaw through steel and concrete. And they gnaw all the time. Rats have to gnaw. Their lives depend on it. Stop gnawing, and their lower teeth grow. Grow until they pierce the brain.

Charles Monk described wild dogs as "the great unmentioned hardship" of travel in the East. But rats are a greater hardship. Dogs can certainly be vicious, but they are also independent. They scavenge alone and attack alone. Not rats. Rats hunt in packs. Rats go through the world in swarms. And a swarm of rats can inflict a lot of damage. A swarm can eat you alive. It can strip your bones in minutes.

I remembered Poe's description of a rat attack: "They pressed—they swarmed upon me in ever accumulating heaps. They writhed upon my throat; their cold lips sought my own; I was stifled by their thronging presence...."

I had to stay calm. To take my mind off this foreign presence, I played a game—naming a capital city for each letter in the alphabet. A is for Addis Ababa; B is for Bucharest; C is for Canberra.... But it was no use. Nothing could distract me from that gnawing.

"Leather Lady!" I said in a loud whisper.

The leather lady was a formidable creature. She could handle this situation.

"Leather Lady! Wake up!"

In my mind's eye, I saw her hand snake from under the bedclothes and, fast as lightning, seize this intruder by the throat and hurl it through the window. But there'd be no help from that quarter. The leather lady snored gently. She was fast asleep.

I lay there, bathed in sweat, and thought of Warburton. In Egypt, he also had been wakened by an animal. "As I slowly opened my eyes," he wrote, "I encountered such a sight as almost made me close them again.... Between me and the moonlight stood the gaunt, hog-backed form of a hyena, all bristling with excitement... his large, round, ghastly eyes... glaring upon mine."

A shout from Warburton, and the beast fled. Maybe I should shout, I thought. And then something awful happened. The gnawing stopped. Good Jesus! What did this mean? I couldn't be sure if the rat had had its fill of biscuits and had now left, or had simply tired of sugar and was looking around for something more palatable to eat. My eyes, for instance.

I pulled the sheet over my head. But that only exposed my feet. Damn that sheet. Why did it have to be so short? I would have to decide which I would sacrifice: my lower extremities or my face. But I couldn't make my mind up. The truth was I didn't want to sacrifice either.

I lay there in a state of terror for what seemed like hours. And then, just as day broke, a muezzin burst forth. "God is great," he sang. "There is but one God, *the* God, and there is but one Prophet, *the* Prophet." Almost at once, my terror abated. I wasn't alone.

I had heard this chant many times, and no two were ever the same. Some were brusque; some were gentle; some were sad. Many sounded exasperated, Islam taking a dim view of man's venality. The one I was hearing now, executed by a light tenor, had something of an appeal about it. We were being urged to come to our senses, to open our hearts to God. If we didn't, the muezzin was telling us, we were doomed. What a terrible thing it must be to be doomed. Far more terrible than being eaten by rats.

A second muezzin started up—a bass, this one. And then a third, a baritone. As always happens, the call to prayer had become a kind of canon.

Though the liturgy requires that the faithful pray at daybreak, just when that is exactly is a matter of personal judgment. According to tradition, night becomes day at the precise moment a white hair can be distinguished from a black one. All well and good, I suppose, if all of us possessed the same keen eyesight. But since we don't, unanimity is rare.

In a country more attached to precision, tradition would defer to science, and the national observatory would be asked for its advice. Charts would be constructed and tables drawn up, and ever after, the muezzins would sing every day in unison.

It isn't likely to happen in Turkey, thank God. Not for a while, anyway. Because Turks, however much the modernists would tell you otherwise, don't much care for exactitude. With luck, they never will. The world has a surfeit of order as it is. And I don't see it being any the better for it.

The chants climbed and curled, waned and waxed again. They twisted before folding in upon themselves. This chant is the arabesque set to music, and it must be hell to execute. Some seem more up to it than others, but even the most accomplished must stop to catch their breath. Since many chants are prerecorded, it would be easy to excise these pauses. But the Turks don't bother. It would be too prosaic, too like those reconstructed walls. There's no shame in having to pause for breath, and no shame, either, in decay. Limitation is the human lot. Limitation ending in death. Death is the ultimate limitation. We spring from the earth, and we return to it. Just as those walls had. Until they were grotesquely resurrected.

The Germans that morning looked drunk with sleep. They were wearing their leather suits again. Had they slept in them? I didn't know. When you share a room with two strangers, you take little notice of what they wear to bed. When it came time to retire, all three of us had set about disrobing without so much as glancing up. It was the same this morning. Though awake, I feigned sleep when the leather couple rose to dress. They themselves were no less delicate. When I got up, they pretended to be writing letters.

Their hair was askew and was much in need of washing. People go to the dogs when they're on holiday.

"If you want," I said, "you two can use the shower first."

But they declined my offer.

"We had a shower on the ship," said the leather lady.

They seemed not to care *how* they looked. Or then again, they may simply not have known. Hotels costing three dollars a night may boast rats, but they don't have mirrors. This means you rarely see yourself. Which is no bad thing. Mirrors encourage insecurity. We gaze into them not for the pleasure of seeing ourselves look good, but out of fear that we might look bad, out of fear that we've degenerated since the last time we looked. A lot can happen in ten minutes. And people, it is said, can age in a trice. No, mirrors exert a kind of tyranny, and we're better rid of them. Away from mirrors, the cut of your jib ceases to be of any great concern. It is enough to know that you're reasonably clean.

Avoid mirrors long enough, and you forget what you look like. This can make for a nice surprise. In the bus station yesterday, I saw a face that looked familiar. Who is that? I thought. And then it struck me. I was gazing at my own reflection. I'd lost weight and my hair was longer. And I wasn't frowning—something I do when I'm anxious. I had changed out of all recognition.

The Germans made light of the rat incident. I had imagined it, they said. Until I pointed to the empty packet of biscuits. And then they said it had probably been a cat. Until I pointed to the rat droppings. And then they said rats never harm anyone. But I knew that to be nonsense, so I moved to another hotel. I don't mind hardship, but when I go to bed at night, I like to think that I'll wake up whole.

This latest hotel had once been the best in Trabzon, I was told. But like much else in this city, it had seen better days. The carpet on the stairs was threadbare, birds nested in the chimneys, and the restaurant smelled like a crypt. The front door needed glass, the floors creaked, and the lobby lay deep in dust. The elevator, the telephone, the television—none of them worked. And neither did the windows in my room. Open one and the other slammed shut; close one and the other fell open. I put it down to sympathetic magic.

Another curiosity was the plumbing. At night, a dribbling

tap kept me awake. But in the mornings, the dribbling stopped—stopped when I could have used a dribble. There was nothing now in which to wash. Not a day passed but something else didn't fail to function. The hotel was falling apart. It was all rather sad.

"How did you sleep?" the owner would ask when he'd see me in the mornings. "Did the tap keep you up?"

Thin and red-faced, he was a nice man, and I knew these dwindling standards weighed heavily on him. He spent all his time making emergency repairs. It was a losing battle, as he must have known. Very soon now, this hotel that once had been the pride of Trabzon would collapse about his ears.

"The tap?" I would say. "It didn't drip at all. I slept very well."

But this he couldn't believe. If the tap hadn't ruined my sleep, then something else must have. "Did the window fall open?" "Did the bulb fail?" "Was the mattress too hard?" One question after another. There was no reassuring him.

"The old days," he would say. "If only you were here in the old days."

But for all its failings, I liked this place. It didn't have rats.

"I haven't seen a rat in years," said the owner. It's possible, I suppose, that he hadn't looked very hard. But that was something I didn't dwell on.

Most of those staying here were soccer fans from Ireland. They looked disgruntled—unhappy about their loss—and they spoke of going home. Some had already gone—which was why I'd been able to get a room. There were Russians here, too. Like the Poles in Istanbul, they had come to shop for contraband. Peddlers crowded around them when they stepped outside. But the Russians were hard to please. They waved away the proffered shirts and jeans—"No good," they said, "too expensive"—and the peddlers dispersed. But only for a moment. Farther down the street, they set upon the Russians once again, and the bargaining resumed, both parties throwing up their hands in exasperation, each accusing the other of intransigence.

Two of the guests were English—a couple on their honeymoon—and while we might have been expected to speak to one another, we didn't. The English, it is widely believed, travel abroad to get away from one another. But that's only true of some. And that's the problem. How to recognize these people? One can't. So the English keep to themselves. Just in case.

I kept my distance, too—even though both of them seemed very nice. I liked the man particularly. The morning I arrived, the water had been turned off and, towards evening, the owner and I were chatting when the Englishman approached with a question.

"Will there be water anytime soon?" he asked politely.

"Not until next week," said the owner, winking in my direction.

"Fine," said the Englishman, not batting an eye.

The next day, the three of us ate lunch on the terrace: they at one table and me at another. Feet apart. It would have been easy to look up and say something, and yet I shrank from doing so. I thought of Alexander Kinglake feeling safe in the middle of the Sinai when—"the horror!"—there hove into view another Briton.

"As we approached each other," he wrote in 1844, "it became with me a question whether we should speak. I thought it likely that the stranger would accost me, and in the event of his doing so, I was quite ready to be as sociable and chatty as I could be according to my nature; but still I could not think of anything particular I had to say to him. . . . The traveler, perhaps, felt as I did, for, except as we lifted our hands to our caps, and waved our arms in courtesy, we passed each other quite as distantly as if we had passed in Pall Mall."

The waiter mentioned the two Britons several times, but I pretended not to understand. He kept piling rolls on my plate, and I, not wanting to hurt his feelings, kept eating them. Which was his signal to give me more. At one stage, the manager, fearing for his profits, ordered him to stop. But the Turk will not be dictated to, and the rolls kept coming. The meal became a contest to determine which was greater: my appetite or his kindness. He was risking his job for a stranger.

I thought he had forgotten the honeymooners when he called to a man who had just sat down. There followed an exchange in Turkish, at the end of which the man came to my table.

"I have good news," he said. "You see those people? They are from your country."

I blushed deeply. The honeymooners, who overheard this, blushed deeply, too. We grinned sheepishly at one another.

"Are you going to Erzurum?" the woman asked.

"At some point, yes. And you?"

"Today at twelve. Do you think the bus will leave on time?"

"They usually do."

She glanced at her watch.

"It's almost ten," she said to her husband. "Let's go to the station now. Just in case."

Just in case the bus left two hours early? It seemed unlikely, but the English, and I'm no exception, have a keen sense of the insecurity of things. Be prepared for everything is their philosophy. Play it safe.

They got to their feet.

"Enjoy Trabzon," said the man.

"I will," I said.

It wasn't much of an exchange. There was so much else we might have talked about: our experiences in Turkey, our lives·in

England. But neither they nor I felt up to it, so we lifted our hands to our caps—figuratively—and waved our arms in courtesy. And then we parted. Sometimes, I can't help thinking, being English is a curse.

There was a second parting that afternoon, this one involving the Germans. They were headed for the Syrian border. Or so they said. They were sure to change their plans before they got there. They seemed a bit sad about leaving. To lighten the mood, I told them about a hotel I'd stayed in in Munich. There was a card on the bedside table. "GUESTS ARE ADVISED," it said in splendid Gothic capitals, "THAT BREAKFAST IS COMPULSORY."

But they only looked confused.

"I don't understand," said the leather lady. "Everyone should eat a breakfast."

"You don't get the joke?" I asked.

She looked disapproving. For her departure, she was wearing a crash helmet and looked more formidable than ever. Even the normally inquisitive Turkish children kept their distance.

"So," she said. "Now you have a sense of humor."

But so did she—however much she might have wished she didn't. When I suggested that she might find a sidecar more comfortable than riding pillion, she referred me to her massive thighs.

"It would have to be a very big sidecar," she said.

I felt lonely when they left and wished I'd asked their names and address. But to do so would have violated the rules for such encounters: be as intimate as you like, but on one condition—the intimacy must remain anonymous. It's better that way. Mention of names puts people on their guard.

For something to do, I went to have my hair cut. The barber took one look at me and summoned his apprentice, a boy of sixteen. A shrewd move, this. Tourists were known to be demanding. In the event of my complaining, he could blame the boy's inexperience.

The apprentice quailed when he saw me. And then he steeled himself.

"Do you want to look like an American?" he asked.

I said I didn't. It's not that I didn't care to look like an American. But whereas I knew what Americans looked like, I couldn't be sure that he did.

As he set to work, the shop filled with spectators. However busy Turks might be, they can't resist a spectacle, and this promised to be a good one. They craned to get a better view of me, one man craning so much that he lost his balance and came crashing down on the man in front of him. I've never seen such interest. I began to wonder if they hadn't been misled. What did they think they had come here to see? A beheading?

The boy continued working, removing what seemed an inordinate amount of hair. Several times I thought him finished and began to get up. But always he'd ease me into the chair again, and his exertions would resume. It was his intention, apparently, to keep going until the results were entirely to his satisfaction. I could only hope that he didn't first run out of hair.

The shop boasted an electric hair dryer—an antiquated thing—but everything else was manual. On the wall in front of me, pride of place was given to a picture of the Trabzon soccer side that, more than a decade earlier, had beaten Liverpool. Trabzon had not seen glory like it since the days of the Byzantine emperors. But its triumph, like all triumphs, was short-lived. Just three weeks later, Liverpool had its revenge, trouncing Trabzon by three goals to one.

Everyone I met in Trabzon was soccer mad. Perhaps they thought that, were Trabzon ever to rise again, it would not be as an empire, but as a power in the world of sports.

"What club do you support?" the apprentice asked.

I was asked this question repeatedly in Trabzon, and at first I had answered truthfully. I didn't support a club, I said; soccer doesn't interest me. But this provoked such incredulity, I had begun to lie. Asked now which club I supported, I sang the praises of Tottenham.

It was a risky claim to make, and more than once my deceit came close to being discovered. There were references to division titles and White Hart Lane—Tottenham's home turf, apparently—and Wembley and F.A. cups—none of which I knew anything about.

There was another close shave now, the apprentice mentioning a certain Hoddle.

"Hoddle who?" I said.

"Charlie Hoddle. One of the best players in the world." And then he laughed. "As if you didn't know."

There was a brief pause when tea arrived, and then the boy set to work again. He chopped and chopped, and I did nothing to stop him. I was past caring.

It's a disaster, I thought. But so what? I'll wear a hat until it grows back.

At last, the dreaded scissors were laid to rest, and my hair—what little remained of it—was combed into place. He was done.

"What do you think?" he said, handing me a mirror.

It was several seconds before I could force myself to look. And when I did, my heart skipped a beat. Wonder of wonders. I looked presentable! I looked fine! The boy had done a first-rate job.

"You're very good," I told him.

"Today, yes," he said. "I'm wearing this."

He pointed to a small silver box hanging from a chain around his neck.

"What is it?" I said.

"It's a charm. It brings me luck."

Trabzon brought lots of people luck. The next morning, I spotted the clashing Lockes strolling in the plaza. Not that they were clashing now. Hand in hand, they were. Gazing into each other's eyes. Mr. Locke said something, and his wife laid her head upon his shoulder. And then she spoke, and the two of them roared with laughter. It was nothing short of a miracle, and my admiration for this city soared. If it could bring together the warring Lockes, then Trabzon was capable of anything.

chapter 4

The bus for Erzurum didn't disappoint. It was scheduled to leave at one o'clock, and at one it left. On the dot. I *so* like machines that do what's expected of them.

The bus looked splendid. A border of tassels ran along the windshield, and the word *mashallah*—God permitting—was printed on the dashboard. A talisman and a picture of a rock star hung from the rearview mirror, while on the ceiling, someone had painted two female eyes: alluring, seductive, fatal.

Erzurum is less than 200 miles from Trabzon, but because one has to cross a mountain range to get there, it is a journey of some eight hours. We left the coast and drove through a wandering valley planted with peppers and plums and apricots. Along the side of the road, hazelnuts lay drying in the sun. The bus crossed a stone bridge and began to climb. We entered a dark forest. Northern Turkey gets lots of rain and is famous for its timber: oak and beech and walnut. Up, up, we went, the transmission straining, until all around us stood the jagged peaks of the Pontic Alps.

A rockslide delayed our progress briefly, and we climbed out to stretch our legs. From somewhere below us came the sound of falling water. Then another sound—bleating—and a boy came into view, driving before him a flock of unruly goats.

"Where do you live?" I asked him.

"Up there," he said, pointing to a cottage clinging to a crag. It looked as precarious as a bird's nest.

Under way again, we climbed until the oaks began to thin. Until there were no oaks. Just pine trees. And then not even pines. We were above the timberline. There was no vegetation at all. Just a long strip of low cloud pierced here and there by granite outcrops looking like tonsured monks.

We descended briefly, climbed a ridge, then descended again. And that's how it was—up and down, up and down—for most of the afternoon. The road wound through long canyons and plunging gorges, past rivers and cataracts. It was superbly Gothic! And then, towards evening, the engine relaxed, and we eased down into an open valley and entered a parched plain. We had reached the windswept highlands of eastern Anatolia.

After the vertical wonders of the Pontic Alps, that plain was a bit of a shock. It was vast. Too vast. It spread in all directions. The scale is wrong, I found myself thinking. Space in this quantity, while it might compel respect, could never inspire affection.

Compounding the plateau's size was its emptiness. A bleaker place would be hard to imagine. Aside from the occasional low hill and stretch of scrub, there was nothing here. No trees. No houses. Worst of all, no people. Just this sprawling void burned yellow by the sun, a yellow Melville described as the color of lions in menageries.

When the rains came, the yellow would recede. But sometimes they didn't come. Or they failed to come in sufficient quantity. And when that happened, the barrenness endured—fixed and immune to challenge.

There was nothing on this plain to relieve the eye and even less to lift the spirit. Just looking at it made me weary. And melancholy. I was glad when the sun set. Even gladder when we got to Erzurum. Crossing that plateau, I imagined our bus getting smaller and smaller. Who knows? One more hour out there, and we might have dwindled to nothing.

Erzurum seemed at something of a loss when I explored it the next morning. And then I remembered that this was Sunday. The western weekend introduced by Ataturk strikes no chord in the bosom of rural Turks. The high point of *their* week is Friday, the Moslem Sabbath. By contrast, Sunday's newly sanctioned leisure confuses them. Those who choose to toil seem halfhearted about it—though not nearly so halfhearted as those who elect to take their ease. Turks are not very good at killing time. Even when they're sedentary, there is a restlessness about them. It shows in the way they draw on their cigarettes, drum their fingers, and worry their beads. They are too alert a people to see much merit in relaxation.

Some shops were open—butcher shops, camera shops, shops full of goatskins—and others were closed: clothes shops, pastry shops, pharmacies. And it was a pharmacy I needed most just then. My head hurt and my nose ran. I was getting a cold. I had to have aspirin.

I found Erzurum to be glum and unattractive. For a time a staging post for caravans making their way to Persia—and briefly the capital of Turkish Armenia—it must once have been an exciting place. Not so now. Local tradition has it that the Garden of Eden existed nearby. Is it this that explains the town's lugubriousness? Its proximity to the place where man discovered shame?

It doesn't help, either, that much of the town is constructed of concrete: concrete office buildings, concrete apartment blocks, even several crude concrete mosques. Concrete is an unsatisfactory building material. It's porous, which means it ages badly. But worse than that, it ages rapidly. Builders have utilized concrete for over a century, but for all that, it's quintessentially modern. It is cheap and malleable—when it's wet, that is—and requires little skill to use. Structures made of concrete can be assembled quickly, which may be why they never look as if they'll last. There's something provisional about them, and they make a place look less than settled.

Erzurum has lots of barracks and training fields. It is a garrison town, which means that many of the 300,000 souls who call this home do so only for a time. The soldiers who account for much of its population come here for basic training. Once they've been versed in the rudiments of war, they are posted elsewhere: to Kars to repel what used to be the Soviets; to Doubayazit to face down Iran; to Diyarbakir to fend off Syria.

This endless coming and going gives Erzurum something of the quality of a holiday resort—though with none of the resort's amenities. The young soldiers who wander its streets look displaced and miserable. Listless and bored and missing home, they loiter in the teahouses. And when loitering becomes intolerable, they take to the streets again, stumbling about with that wretched aimlessness peculiar to people who are killing time.

It distressed me to see unhappiness on such a scale: young boys with shaved heads and ill-fitting uniforms and so new to soldiering, some of them, that leaving the tea shops, they forgot their hats.

"You're forgetting something," I called after one of them. But he didn't hear.

"Don't worry," said a man. "He'll be back."

And he was. Not three minutes later. Red with embarrassment and out of breath and looking close to tears. How young he seemed. He was just a child.

The next morning, my cold had worsened. My head pounded more fiercely than ever, and my throat hurt. I began to wonder if I wasn't getting the flu.

"Whatever it is, it's nothing very serious," I told myself. "I'll be fine if I take it easy."

I ate a large lunch in the hope it might revive my strength. But the results were ambiguous. I felt a little stronger, yes, but now my stomach hurt. Perhaps the meal had been a mistake. What was the maxim? Feed a cold and starve a fever? Or starve a cold and *feed* a fever? I could never remember. By eating, I may have harmed myself irrevocably.

By evening, my tonsils had become inflamed, and it hurt to breathe. Now an even graver possibility presented itself. Suppose what I had was more serious than the flu. Suppose I was getting pleurisy. Or bronchitis. Or even pneumonia.

Until that moment, I had thought of this ailment as nothing more than a minor nuisance, a discomfort, a setback requiring that I slacken my pace or, at the very worst, spend a day or two in bed. Now, I had to wonder if I mightn't be forced to cut my journey short. I had to wonder—yes, I was yielding to panic—if I mightn't end my days in this wretched place!

Few things are more demoralizing than falling ill abroad. And what makes it so is not being sick, as such, or being far from home. (Though in combination, neither is very pleasant.) It's being forced to realize that you're less than smart.

The traveler prides himself on his acumen, on his ability to cope. He congratulates himself on how well he's doing. He's on schedule. He's within his budget. He's avoided trouble. His health is holding up. All of this is cause for celebration. You begin to think that you might be a traveler, after all. You begin to believe that you might be competent. And then, out of the blue, this happens. You're ill—flat on your back—and your self-assurance is exposed as one big sham.

I had to decide what to do. Would I yield and take to my bed? Or would I resist and tough it out? The latter seemed the better course. At least it left one with a semblance of pride. I would prove to my body I was more than a match for it.

87

We pitted wills rather a lot, my body and I. Several times on this trip, I'd gone without socks (good for the feet); gone without meals (good for the stomach); and gone without sleep (good for the soul). I liked the idea of controlling my body—dictating what it should have and how it should behave. Hardening it, making it strong, preparing it for the rigors that lay ahead. (That rigors *did* lie ahead, I didn't doubt for a moment.)

Was I something of a puritan? Yes, I suppose I was. But not all the time. My puritanism was intermittent. A week of abstinence was followed by a month of self-indulgence. There was no end to the ways one might punish the body—and no end to the pleasure to be got from doing so. But it was, I found, a hollow pleasure. A far cry from the joys of hedonism. My self-abnegation was only part puritanical. It was more an assertion of authority. I didn't despise my body. I simply wanted it to know just which of us was boss.

I don't understand people who hate their bodies. I mean, *really* hate them. Like the stylites, the Christian ascetics of the early Middle Ages. In Istanbul, I visited Istiniye, where, for three decades, St. Daniel had lived on top of a pillar. He died up there, this man who disdained the creature comforts. Those followers who went to fetch him down found him half-eaten by worms and horribly contorted. To get him into a coffin, they had first to straighten him. And as they did so, someone recounted, "his bones creaked so loudly that we thought his body would be shattered."

Those stylites! What was one to make of their austerities? They fasted. They scourged themselves. They wore hair shirts. They slept on nails. Anything to tame the flesh and sanctify the spirit. What carnal loathing! No abasement was too great. They refused to wash. They declined to speak. They wrapped themselves in chains. They ate manure. They stood on burning coals. And these punishments didn't always stop with death. One insisted he be buried on a busy street so that everyone—"even the dogs and goats"—might have the satisfaction of walking over him. Were they saintly or were they mad? Were they both?

The next day, I was sicker than ever. I'll have to see a doctor, I thought. And then I decided that, no, I couldn't. A doctor was beyond my means. To recover my health, I'd have to devise my own cure.

I turned for help to my travel books. Thomas Manning, when his throat hurt, ate currant jelly. It was highly efficacious, said the first Englishman to visit Lhasa—unless the soreness was accompanied by palpitations. When that happened, he advised that one eat a turnip.

James Holman, who despite being blind became known as "the greatest traveler of all time," abstained from food when fever struck and filled his head with happy thoughts.

Charles Waterton, the naturalist, was more extreme. In the jungles of South America, he treated fever as he treated everything else—by reaching for his lancet. Waterton was also a champion of that other staple of Victorian medicine, the poultice. His favorite contained boiled cow dung. To work, he said, it was crucial that the dung be fresh.

So what would it be? Currant jelly? Bloodletting? Or cow dung? I opted for the jelly, but hard as I looked, Erzurum didn't yield any. Instead, I tried to eat some soup. Impossible. My hand trembled so much, I couldn't raise the spoon.

"You're not looking well," said the waiter. "I'll get you some tea."

And that's what I lived on for the next four days: glass after glass of tea. So many glasses, it's a wonder I didn't die of tannin poisoning. Gazing into that amber liquid, I never failed to remember that line of Kinglake's: "And soon there was tea before us, with all its unspeakable fragrance." Tea *is* unspeakably fragrant. Nothing else comes close.

Life without tea would be unimaginable. I'm not surprised that many travelers wouldn't think of going anywhere without it. Holman crossed Russia "provided with tea and sugar for the whole journey . . . and thus, having also with me a teapot, cups, etc., I was quite independent of the accidental and inadequate entertainment the post-houses could furnish, with the exception of hot water."

Burnaby found tea "an absolute necessity when riding across the steppes in mid-winter, and [it] is far superior in heat-giving properties to any wines or spirits. In fact, a traveller would succumb to the cold on the latter when the former will save his life."

Turkey is a good country for the tea lover; I know of no other that loves tea more. It is rare to see a Turk without a glass of tea. At home, the samovar is ever on the boil, while at work, he need only raise a finger and tea is procured from a vendor, his trays, suspended on strings from either hand, looking like the scales of justice.

And then there are the ubiquitous teahouses. The nicer ones occupy courtyards, the tables set along white walls and shaded by the leaves of a plane tree. Tea is served in a small, gently fluted glass. And beneath the glass is a saucer—more a dish, really, decorated with alternating smudges of red and gold.

Each glass comes with two cubes of sugar. And that presented me with a problem. One cube provided insufficient sweetness, while two provided a little too much. It meant having to break a cube in half. Which was never easy. Eventually, I devised the solution of biting it in two, dropping one half in my glass and swallowing the other.

Ah, the pleasure of watching that sugar melt. The warmth when you held the glass. The happiness of that first sip. So delicious.

(In taste, Turkish tea resembles Darjeeling.) The pace at which you drink is entirely a matter for yourself. You can take all day if you want to. Having bought a glass of tea, you now have tenure. Time passes quickly in teahouses. Without realizing it, I once spent five hours in one. When I glanced at my watch, I thought, Uh-oh. The bloody thing's gone haywire.

Pound for pound, tea contains as much caffeine as coffee, and it certainly is a stimulant. But a beneficent stimulant. While coffee charges one with a bogus, edgy energy, tea invigorates. It restores. The therapeutic effects of tea have not been sufficiently investigated. It revitalizes, yes, but its effects are more than physical. Tea soothes. It knits up the raveled sleeve of care. It firms the will. Milton, it is said, drank coffee while writing *Paradise Lost,* tea while working on *Paradise Regained.*

"Thank God for tea!" cried Sydney Smith. "What would we do without it?" What, indeed? Tea is my opiate. Booze is fine when you've something to celebrate. But disappointment requires a gentler medicine. There's just one thing to do when loss comes calling: you put the kettle on.

Dr. Johnson drank so much tea, he tells us, his kettle "scarcely had time to cool." Ten cups one after another were nothing to this man. He once drank *sixteen* cups, prompting his hostess to wonder if he shouldn't use a basin.

In vino veritas, it has been remarked. Though I doubt it. No one prevaricates quite like a drunk. Tea, though, is another matter. Tea makes for intimacy, and intimacy is sacred. Drinking tea, I could never be anything but frank. A cup of tea is like a Bible.

My favorite teahouse in Erzurum was near the market. An unprepossessing place, it was dark and grubby and thick with flies. But it hardly mattered. It was full of old men—white-haired fellows with shining eyes set in latticed skin. Like olives nestling in leaves of phyllo dough.

These ancients sat hunched over water pipes. They didn't speak, and they didn't stir. Did their pipes not bubble from time to time, you'd have said they were dead. Outside, Erzurum was all noise and motion. Horse-drawn carts thundered past, and vendors yelled to one another, but the ancients didn't notice. In a sense, they *were* dead. Absorbed in their smoking, they were dead to the world.

Nor did they notice the man who primed their pipes. A short fellow with a beard—nicotine had yellowed the hair around his mouth—he moved among the smokers with a saucepan full of burning coals. One could feel their heat when he passed. The handle must have been hellishly hot, yet I never saw him wear a glove. What enviable indifference.

I wanted to be indifferent, too. I wanted to forget I was sick. Or, if I couldn't forget, I wanted not to care. How could I do that? I'd need patience, wouldn't I? A lot of patience. And I had none at all. Even as I thought these things, I could feel myself growing restless.

"You've seen enough of this place," said part of me. "Let's go."

"Be quiet," said another part. "Learn to be still."

My head began to throb. I'd now been sick for four days, but instead of getting better, I was getting worse. I stumbled back to the hotel and struggled into bed. My excursion to the teahouse had exhausted me. I hated myself for being this weak. Though that was hardly fair. There is no disgrace in being ill. Sickness could fell anyone—even a person as tough as Burnaby.

Burnaby could bend a poker with his bare hands, but even he—with his "small stock of medicines . . . in the event of any illness on the road"—proved no match for Turkey.

"I had suffered great pain during the last two marches," he complained. "My legs seemed to have lost all their strength; I had great pain in the head and back. My pulse was beating very rapidly. It intermitted."

I read this with mounting dread. One didn't like to see a man of Burnaby's strength succumb like this. If it could happen to him, what hope was there for the likes of me? Perhaps if he slept a few hours . . .

But the next morning, Burnaby was feeling worse. "I found myself so weak that I could barely raise my head from the pillow. . . . I lay all day racked by pain, and half devoured by insects."

Burnaby was finally diagnosed as having rheumatic fever. Or, as his doctor put it: "Your heart is out of order."

I stayed in bed all day. A bad idea, it turned out. I regress when I'm supine for any length of time. I became irrational, yielding more and more to fancy. I fell asleep and had a dream: I was being buried in Erzurum's equivalent of potter's field. The only mourners were the old men from the teahouse, still puffing on their water pipes.

"This is a fearful waste of money," said one of them. "Why don't we simply feed him to the dogs?"

I woke in a sweat.

Being indisposed like this was additionally miserable because I was ill at a time when I needed all my resources for the task at hand. I had come here to write and, for almost a week now, I'd written nothing at all. Not even a diary entry. So, to my fever and sore throat and burning lungs was added another torment: the feeling that I was falling short professionally.

Even well, one feared that, for all one's exertions, one was not seeing enough; or that one was seeing the wrong things; or that one was seeing the *right* things, but drawing the wrong conclusions. When one was ill, this fear was compounded many times over.

I got up to take a shower. But I'd only started when the

water dwindled to a slow trickle and then ceased altogether. I'd looked forward to this shower all day, and suddenly I'd had enough. Whatever the cost, I had to get my strength back. I'd go and see a doctor.

Kirim, the man who owned this place, recommended his brother.

"He's very good," he said. "He trained in London."

"Will he charge much?"

"Not if you tell him you're a friend of mine."

His brother lived on the other side of town, and Kirim suggested I take a taxi.

"Look," he said, taking my elbow. "There's one outside."

With great care, he placed me in the backseat. And then he got behind the wheel.

"This is your taxi?"

He nodded.

"A sideline," he explained.

My examination was not extensive. The doctor, a tall man with silver hair and a Rolex watch, sounded my chest and peered down my throat. And then, looking grave—for form's sake, I can only imagine—he announced his diagnosis.

"You have a bad viral infection," he said. "You're going to need lots of rest and lots of penicillin. I'll give you a prescription."

He put away his stethoscope.

"Better put your shirt on," he said, grinning. "We don't want you to catch a cold."

I'd been here all of five minutes.

"Don't you have to do tests or anything?" I asked.

He shook his head.

"Yours is the fourth case I've seen today. There's a lot of this about."

He refused to take any money.

"But I want you to do something for me," he said. "When you're back in London, give my regards to St. Guy's."

He handed me my prescription.

"Is there a pharmacy near here?" I asked.

"Ask my brother," he said. "He'll know of one."

Kirim drove me to a shop so brightly lighted it made me squint. The staff of three was very deferential, rising to their feet when we entered, offering us chairs, and inquiring if we'd care for tea.

"Weren't they nice to us?" I said back in the taxi.

"They had to be," he said, grinning. "They work for me."

"You mean—"

"That's my shop."

"As well as the hotel and the taxi, you own a pharmacy?"

"I have to. I'm raising three children."

He suggested I eat something, so we stopped at a small restaurant. Now that I'd seen a doctor, I felt a little better, and I managed to eat a salad. But when I tried to pay, Kirim raised a hand.

"No need," he said.

"Don't tell me you own this place, too."

He laughed.

"Not quite. I have a half interest."

This was a man of many parts. He reminded me of Pooh-Bah in *The Mikado*—"The Lord-High-Everything-Else" who was first lord of the Treasury, lord chief justice, commander in chief, lord high admiral, archbishop, and lord mayor all rolled into one. A genial fellow, he was short and fat and lacked a neck. He looked like a Toby mug.

I spent the rest of the week in bed, husbanding my strength. Kirim often came to visit.

The purpose of these visits was twofold: to offer sympathy

and to talk about his own health. He had gallstones, which, he claimed, were sure to prove the death of him. Those he had managed to pass he kept in a jar in his office.

"There are dozens of them," he said. "All as big as kidney beans."

Besides gallstones, he had a bleeding ulcer, a perforated eardrum, and a hernia, each of which he described at enormous length. I tried several times to get him to change the subject, but he wouldn't be deflected. There's no one vainer than a man with health problems.

"You don't sound well at all," I said once.

"I'm not. I work too hard. I rarely see my family anymore. I'm never home."

"You should see your family."

"I know. But I also have to work. I have to make a living."

"You can make a living without working day and night. Why have you got that pharmacy? Or the taxi? You could live quite well off this hotel."

"Are you serious?" he said. "It's falling apart."

It was called The Sultan, and it *was* a bit dilapidated. I had stayed in a "Sultan" in Istanbul, and it had been dilapidated, too. In Istanbul, I'd also stayed in a "Kismet" and a "Topkapi," and I knew now to expect little of places whose names evoked an exotic past. Conditions in even the most extravagantly named of these hotels were rarely more than primitive. Names like Sultan were not invoked to suggest linkage. They were intended only as compensation.

Kirim was full of plans. He was going to renovate The Sultan, he said. And when that was done, he'd buy another taxi. And then, he'd buy a bus. He was determined to be rich.

"I may move to Germany," he said. "There's nothing to do

here. It's dead. Especially in winter. Snow as high as your waist. And wolves."

"Real wolves?"

"Real wolves. Hungry wolves. Go out and you risk being eaten. It's bad for business."

One day, I left bed briefly, and he and I went to the teahouse I liked so much, the one with the old men. The ancients were sitting as they always sat: hunched over their water pipes, silent, immobile, completely absorbed.

"Look at them," I said. "They're extraordinary. I'd love to be like that."

"Don't fool yourself," he said, sounding angry. "Those people may be picturesque, but that's all they are. I'm the new Turkey; they're the old. Were it left to them, we'd still be living in the Middle Ages."

I might have stayed in bed longer if Kirim hadn't come to my room one morning and made the astonishing announcement that Erzurum, just then, was full of writers.

"What do you mean, 'full,'" I said.

"I mean full. There must be at least one writer in every hotel in town."

"How many hotels is that?"

"Twenty? Thirty?"

"You mean Turkish writers, don't you?"

"No," said Kirim. "Europeans. Americans."

This was most disturbing.

"What are they doing?" I said. Though I hardly dared to ask.

"Doing?" he said. "Writing, I suppose."

"About what?"

He looked surprised.

"About Turkey, of course."

"But they can't be," I said. "*I'm* writing about Turkey."

I had chosen to come here because *no one* wrote about Turkey. Not recently, anyway. Nowadays, people wrote about Provence and Tuscany and small towns in Portugal. Those, that is, who were disciples of Henry James. There was another breed—the venturesome: the sort who went where few had gone before. But they wrote about Borneo and Zaire and Bolivia. I was staking a claim to the middle ground: places the Henry James disciples would consider much too dangerous, and the venturesome would dismiss as far too safe.

Now, if Kirim could be believed, dozens of others were staking similar claims. And right under my nose. I didn't only have a virus to contend with. I had COMPETITION!

I couldn't stay in bed now. I had to get up. I had to press on. There was work to be done. And the sooner I did it the better.

The story was apocryphal, it turned out. There were *three* writers in town: English journalists on their way to the Iraqi border. But it didn't matter. That story had served a purpose. I was still a little groggy, but for all that, I was back on my feet.

I washed my clothes and took a shower, but instead of washing my hair—I was afraid I'd compound my infection—I put gel in it and combed it off my forehead. It made me look quite nasty. And do you know something? I acted nasty all that day.

I snapped at the waiter during lunch, and later I snapped at a bootblack. "*Yok,*" I said fiercely when he asked for the fourth time if he might polish my shoes. Are hairstyles destiny? I really don't know. But I will tell you this: in the future, I'll be careful how I comb my hair.

When I told Kirim I was off to Kars, he offered to book me a seat on a bus.

"I know a good travel agency," he said.

Really? I said. And was he in any way associated with this estimable firm?

Well, yes, he said, looking sheepish. He was. He'd invested a small amount of money in it. But if I was unhappy . . .

No, no, I assured him. I was perfectly happy. If this firm could get me to Kars in reasonable comfort, he should proceed with all due haste.

"And I'll need a taxi," I said. "To get to the bus station. I don't suppose you'd know of one, would you?"

He grinned.

"Don't worry," he said. "I know just the man."

"You're sure? Getting in touch with him won't be any trouble?"

"No trouble at all," he said. "I see him all the time."

chapter 5

There are pictures of Ataturk everywhere one goes in Turkey, but if quantity is what you seek, then go to Erzurum and head for the bus station.

Such pictures!

Ataturk young; Ataturk old; Ataturk in middle age.

Ataturk at work; Ataturk at play; Ataturk lost in thought.

Ataturk in uniform; Ataturk in mufti; Ataturk in coat and tails.

Ataturk looking dour; Ataturk looking downcast; Ataturk, his thoughts, perhaps, on the afterlife, looking skyward.

Ataturk as a young Olivier; Ataturk as a mature George Sanders; Ataturk as an old Ralph Richardson.

Dozens and dozens of pictures, and no two of them the same. What a protean figure he must have been!

Curiously, in not one of these pictures does Ataturk smile. But then, even by his own account, he was a gloomy fellow. "How could I be otherwise?" he liked to ask. "Isn't modernizing a nation a serious business?"

No doubt it is, but Ataturk may have been *too* serious. When a kangaroo court convicted his best friend of plotting to kill him— the evidence was never more than nebulous—it was Ataturk who signed the death warrant. And once, he refused to see a jilted lover, even though she was dying of consumption. The woman blew her brains out.

Ataturk affected not to mind. He had a job to do. And this, if anything, is the Turkish flaw: this single-mindedness, this refusal to let anything distract from the task at hand. The Turk is tenacious to a fault.

Two military policemen patrolled the terminus as I waited for my bus. Armed with machine guns, they looked quite nasty. But who toting a gun doesn't? Put an automatic in the hands of a nun, and she, too, will inspire a measure of wariness.

They walked about, these two, checking papers, scanning faces, subjecting everything to scrutiny. What was disconcerting about them was not their being vigilant as much as the pleasure it gave them. *They were having an awfully good time.* Watching them made me feel uneasy. Power is like alcohol. It goes directly to the head. And it leaves one craving more.

On the bus, a woman tried to swap tickets with me. Hers cost 10,000 lira; mine, 25,000. "Trust me," she said. But for once I didn't. I didn't fancy being turned off this bus in the middle of nowhere.

The driver, moving his lips, counted us repeatedly. According to the manifest, there should have been forty of us. According to him, we numbered forty-one. That was the first time he counted. The second time, we had grown to forty-two; and the third time to forty-three. The fourth time, we had dwindled dramatically. We were now down to a mere thirty-eight.

That was because several people had left to buy sandwiches, said a woman.

"How many?" said the driver.

But she didn't know. Not that it mattered. As quickly as people were getting off, others were getting on. Despairing, finally, the driver handed the manifest to his assistant.

"Here," he said. "You have a go."

But the assistant, though he moved his lips as fiercely as the driver had, fared no better, so they sent for the man at the ticket counter. The manifest was passed from hand to hand, and then the ticket agent asked for silence. A fraud had been committed, he said, and the bus wouldn't leave until the perpetrator had been brought to book.

One by one, he checked our tickets, writing the numbers on a piece of paper. And then he scratched his head. The numbers still didn't tally. The assistant offered the view that the whole thing was a mystery, and the driver agreed. We were wasting time, he said. We needed to get going.

But the agent wouldn't hear of it. Someone on this bus had a ticket he hadn't paid for. And he meant to find that person. Even if it took all day. The driver pleaded. The assistant pleaded. Even the passengers pleaded. But the agent was adamant. He had a job to do. He couldn't neglect his duty.

Normally, I admire people who stick to their guns, but this man was getting tiresome. The driver must have thought so, too, because he grabbed him and forced him off the bus. And then we were roaring out of the terminus with the agent in hot pursuit, his face so full of rage it made me catch my breath.

It was awfully hot on that bus. The air-conditioning, turned on with great ceremony when we left the station, was turned off again ten minutes later.

The person next to me—a young soldier—grinned and asked if I'd let him smoke. His teeth were rotting.

"Go ahead," I said.

His name was Hussein, he had just turned twenty, and he hated the army.

"Turkish soldiers are dirty," he said. "Our clothes are dirty; our food is dirty. Everything is dirty."

By *dirty,* he apparently meant "bad." Later, when describing how tired he was, he said, "Last night, I slept dirty."

Dirtiest of all were his officers.

"The Turkish army has too much discipline," he said, jabbing the air with his fists.

He was returning to Kars after a month in Antalya. His mother was ill, and the army had let him visit her. He missed home a lot.

"I'll bet it's nice in Antalya today," he said wistfully.

He made a show of being stoic, but occasionally his apprehension got the better of him, and he'd look wild for a moment and lean forward in his seat as if he meant to bolt.

He showed me a diary the army had given him when he enlisted. Called *A Soldier's Story,* it described, from what I could gather, the training he would undergo. Inside the back cover was a block of squares, one for every day of the eighteen months he'd spend in uniform.

"Five hundred and fifty days," he said.

Some of the squares had been inked out, but there remained a dismaying number still to go. He pointed to a square far in the future.

"That's the day I finish," he said. "Think of me that day."

A sigh escaped him. It must have seemed an eternity away. He was just a child, and my heart went out to him. I'd have done anything just then to relieve his misery.

It hadn't occurred to him to avoid conscription. Some did, rupturing themselves to win a medical exemption. It's something Turks have been doing for a long time. Burnaby commented on the practice a century ago.

"The operation hurts," he wrote.

In other parts of the empire, the remedies were more extreme. To avoid being drafted, Warburton tells us, "at least two-thirds of the male population of Egypt have deprived themselves of the right eye, or of the forefinger of the right hand." The boat taking him up the Nile had a crew of twelve, seven of whom "were either one-eyed or fore-fingerless."

Hussein ran his hands through his hair. That afternoon, it would be shorn by an army barber, and he was missing it already. He wanted to know if I'd done *my* military service. He grinned when I shook my head.

"Ah," he said, rubbing together finger and thumb. "You paid money."

I tried to explain that, in England, one joined the army only if one wanted to. But this was something beyond his ken. Military service was compulsory in Turkey, and it hadn't occurred to him that elsewhere it might be otherwise. He decided, finally, that I was pulling his leg.

"I get it," he said. "This is a joke."

Such a capital joke that he told the soldier behind him. Who told the soldier behind *him*. They had a good laugh, the three of them. Think of it: a country in which people enlisted only if it suited them. It was too funny for words. Turks are reserved in their laughter, but they value a humorist. Those soldiers pressed apples on me for the rest of the trip.

When he got his discharge, it was Hussein's plan to return to Antalya and marry a tourist.

"I want to leave Turkey," he said. "Turkey is dirty."

He produced an aging slip of paper on which were written three addresses: one in England, one in Belgium, the third in Germany.

"People I met in Antalya," he said. "Friends."

Did he write to these people?

He shook his head.

Did they write to him?

He shook his head again.

He carried this piece of paper, carefully folded, in the back of his wallet. There's no telling what would happen were he to contact these people—and maybe he knew better than to try—but for now, at least, he could think of them as allies. This list was his link with the outside world. A tenuous link, but it made him feel less lonely. It gave him courage.

Without my realizing it, we had left the flat and yellow plain surrounding Erzurum and entered the plain surrounding Kars— just as flat and no less yellow. When the rains came, this plain would transform itself, becoming a vast grazing pasture. But now it lay dormant, its energies dozing below the surface, gathering strength for the massive regeneration that lay ahead.

The trip from Erzurum lasted four hours, during which we didn't see a soul. Where was everyone? Like nature, had they retreated underground as well?

My reception in Kars was an odd one—a series of fierce *yok*s. *Yok* is a splendid invention, and one only wishes that English had a word of its utility. But the effect of quite so many in so short a time—and delivered so emphatically—was nothing if not unnerving.

No one had heard of the hotel I was looking for. It didn't exist, I was told. But I knew someone who had stayed there not a week earlier, I said. Impossible, they insisted. *Yok, yok, yok.* Kars didn't have such a hotel. Not now, not ever.

Mention of the tourist office produced more *yok*s.

"There's no tourist office?"

No, they weren't saying that, they said. A tourist office did exist. But there was no point going there. It had closed for the season. Surely not, I said. This *was* the season. But they were adamant. As was its habit when September rolled around, the tourist office had closed shop.

And, finally, I was told on reaching Kars, I should abandon all hope of going to Ani, the former Armenian capital on the Russian border. No one had gone there in years.

"Are you sure?" I said. "My guidebook . . ."

But they didn't want to hear about my guidebook. Hadn't I heard that the Russians shot anyone who ventured near their frontier? No, Ani was out of the question. *Yok, yok, yok.*

What a disappointment. I had come to Kars for the express purpose of seeing Ani, and now it didn't look as if I would.

"Maybe the chief can help," said Hussein.

"What chief?"

"That's what people call him. I don't know why. But he gets things done. Let's find him."

He didn't look like a chief, this obese man whose neck was so fat, it spilled over his collar like a ruff. He wore a suit with a large patch on one of the knees. His hands were huge and very, very dirty.

But I didn't doubt that here was a man who inspired respect. We found him in a teahouse playing chess. Behind his chair, a gallery of admirers watched in silence. Our way was barred when we tried to speak to him. He was busy, we were told. We would have to wait.

A great clatter of pots and pans issued from a corner where a small boy, partially obscured by a screen, was making tea. Steam from a boiling samovar swirled about him. He put me in mind of the Wizard of Oz.

Those not watching the chief play chess watched a soft-core film on television. During the love scenes, their mouths fell open. Not daring to look away even for a moment, they groped for their tea and their cigarettes. One man was lighting a match when the woman on the screen began to remove her girdle. It burned down and scorched his fingers.

We waited half an hour, during which the chief, who was no chess player, lost one piece after another. The game would have been shorter had his opponent not deliberately prolonged it. For reasons of his own, he wanted the chief to think that his victory had not been easy.

The chief, who spoke only Kurdish, was gracious when Hussein introduced me. After providing me with tea, he said it was always an honor to receive a visitor from England, particularly one so distinguished.

I glanced at Hussein, who was acting as translator.

"Tell him he's very gracious," I said, "but he should understand that I'm just a tourist. I'm not distinguished at all."

Hussein took his time translating this, and when he finished, the chief bowed very low. When he spoke, he sounded more unctuous than ever.

"He says he is honored that you would travel all this way to visit him," said Hussein, "and he asks that you relay his compliments to your queen."

"Tell him I didn't travel all this way to visit him," I said. "I traveled all this way to visit Ani. Which is why I need his help."

Turning to the chief, Hussein now spoke at even greater length, the Kurd, in the meantime, nodding in my direction and beaming like a jack-o'-lantern. When he spoke, the chief's voice broke with emotion.

"He wants you to tell the English people that their friends in Turkey have never forgotten that when they stood alone against the czar, it was the English who came to their assistance. He wants you to assure them—"

"For Christ's sake, Hussein, just what are you telling this man?"

"Exactly what you're telling me."

"You can't be. He's under the impression I'm some kind of dignitary. Make him understand I'm of no importance."

"I'm getting to that," he said.

"Then get to it now. If you aren't careful, you'll land me in jail."

Hussein translated once again, after which the chief, brushing away a tear, said something which Hussein rendered thus: "He says his heart bursts with happiness, and that he'll remember this day for the rest of his life."

I'd had enough of this.

"Hussein!" I said. "I don't know what it is you're doing, but I want you to stop."

"But—"

"But nothing. We're leaving."

The chief got to his feet when I stood up and, still smiling, kissed me on either cheek. And then he embraced me and slapped my back, after which he kissed me again. When he was quite finished, it was the turn of his entourage, all eight of whom hugged me tightly, which was most uncomfortable. Two of them had guns tucked into their trousers.

I didn't need the chief to get me to Ani, it turned out. The next morning, I found the tourist office—not closed and shuttered as I'd been told—but open for business and fully staffed.

"I don't know who you talked to," said one of the officials. "Everyone knows we're here all year."

I'd been misled about Ani, too. People went there all the time. In fact, it was now quite easy. Once, one had needed an armed escort to go to the frontier. But that was a year ago. Back in the Dark Ages. Back when Ivan had an empire and was jealous of his borders.

I loved Kars. It was small and unprepossessing; the roads were treacherous, and the houses were less than mean. But redeeming all was its vigor. Buses tore through the streets; carts tore; people tore; goats tore. In Kars, you had a choice: you tore or you perished.

There was also a rage for sweeping. Merchants swept their shops, and housewives swept their homes. In each case, the detritus was then swept into the street, where a city employee swept it into the gutter. Later, no doubt, another city employee would sweep it someplace else, but for the moment it lay there, attracting an occasional rat. Which was fine with me. As long as rats found nourishment in gutters, they weren't likely to disturb my sleep.

Besides being a ferment of activity, Kars was full of clamor. I wouldn't have thought it possible that so few people could make so much noise. But there it was: from early morning to late at night, Kars was a constant din.

It didn't have much in the way of civilized amenities. But then, it didn't need them. It was a frontier town with a frontier spirit, and its effect on me was tonic. Still enervated by my bout of fever, I strolled through grubby streets lined with grubby houses and felt my strength return. Life in this far-flung outpost can only have been primitive. But it was vivid, too. And splendidly uncouth. Hard to imagine afternoon teas and amateur theatricals in a town like this. Kars had no place for airs and graces. And why should it? What was civilization, after all, but a kind of tyranny?

Kars did my heart good. It was raw and half-formed, the way it was a century ago, probably, and, very likely, the way it would be in a century's time. Kars didn't have the time to cultivate refinement. It was all it could do to survive. Kars was *content* to survive. It had set itself the limited goal of simply getting by. And insofar as it managed this, it was perfectly happy. Of all the places

I'd visited, modest little Kars seemed far and away the most content.

To describe it as modest is not to suggest that it lacked for excitement. Walking through the market one evening, I came upon an altercation. It had to do, from what I was able to glean, with the ownership of a melon. The disputants were two middle-aged men, one of whom, when I chanced upon them, had just cut the disputed fruit in half and kicked it into the street.

At this, the other claimant became enraged and, casting about for a weapon, grabbed a broom and gave his opponent a whack on the head. What struck me as significant was not the whack—which was delivered with no great force and did little harm—but rather the broom. There were other things he might have grabbed: a knife, for example. Or a walking stick, stout enough to be a club and perfect for braining a man.

If, then, it was his intention to inflict serious bodily harm, it cannot be said that he lacked for means. Yet presented with a walking stick, a knife, and a broom, he choose the most harmless of the three. And he did so at a time when he was angry and might have been expected to act irrationally. No, I thought afterwards, the Turk had to be a very steady fellow. Even in a rage, he kept his head.

The two were quickly parted. (That's something else one sees in Turkey, this parting of belligerents.) But too late. They had drawn the notice of the law, and they were bundled, the two of them—along with the broom and both halves of the disputed melon—into a police car.

I didn't like the police in Kars. They had a tendency to act like bullies. Their special pleasure was hounding street vendors. One needed a license to sell from a barrow, and many vendors didn't have one. It made shopping unpredictable. Once, the man who was cooking me a shish kebab was ordered to move his grill, forcing me to follow him two blocks to get my change.

Another day, a fruit seller fleeing the police ran his barrow over my foot. Had he kept on going, he might have got away. Instead, he stopped to apologize, and he was nabbed, the police confiscating his weights and scales. Effectively, this put him out of business, and he followed the police for several blocks, intending, I suppose, to throw himself on their mercy. He never quite summoned the courage.

I found it disturbing. I don't mean the police enforcing the law—which they had every right to do—but rather the glee with which they did it. Like those soldiers checking papers in Erzurum, they weren't just performing a duty. They were doing this for sport. There was about their zeal a suggestion of sadism.

———

The next morning, I headed for the citadel. No. *Headed* is not the word. To *head* somewhere, you need a sense of direction. And I don't have one.

I've despaired of ever finding things. Finding them purposefully, I mean. I rely now on chancing on them. What that comes down to is this: I see a lot of things I don't plan to see and few of the things I *do* plan to see. But the former, I've discovered, are much more interesting, so it all works out in the end.

It would help, I suppose, if I could read a map. Kinglake was always "conning over maps," he tells us. Not me. I can't make head or tail of them. This is one of the reasons I so like Wolff. He avoided maps, too. And he refused to carry a compass. All it did, he said, was compound his confusion.

One didn't really need a map in Kars. Seeing the sights was relatively easy because, in the first place, there are only three; and in the second, all lie within a short distance of one another. This simplified things enormously, and I could only wish that other cities were as sensibly arranged. But since few are, why not make them so? The government that relocates Stonehenge and Kew Gardens and the Brighton Pavilion in the center of London would be doing tourism an enormous service.

As I said, find one of Kars's attractions, and you've found them all. But that's no help until you *do* find one. Which, true to form, I had trouble doing. The citadel is a massive thing, and it sits, high above the town, in plain view of all. But while I had no trouble *seeing* the wretched thing, what I couldn't seem to do was approach it. Every street I took ended in a blank wall or ran into the river or turned suddenly when my goal seemed just within reach and led me back to the center of town. I was on the point of giving up when two soldiers overtook me. With their compact brown heads and their light green uniforms, they resembled hazelnuts that had still to shed their husks.

"The citadel?" they asked.

I nodded, and they told me to follow them.

Chatting happily, they walked ahead of me with their arms linked. Such camaraderie. An army as genial as this one can't pose much of a threat, I thought. Or could it? Perhaps it is the love he bears his fellows that makes the Turkish soldier so formidable. Threaten one, and you threaten all. Isn't that the ultimate camaraderie? A readiness to die for one's friends?

One of the two, a sergeant, spoke good English. Remembering what Hussein had told me, I asked him if he beat his subordinates.

"All the time," he said. "Want to know why?"

One day, he said, a lieutenant accused him of going easy on his men.

"You're not making them soldiers," he complained.

"I try," said the sergeant. "They don't listen to me."

"Ah, but you have to *make* them listen," said the lieutenant. "Let me show you how."

And taking the sergeant behind the gym, he beat him senseless.

"I've no problem now," said the sergeant. "My men respect me."

The citadel was directly above us now. From here, its dark stone walls looked vast and mighty and unassailable. But even a fortress as big as this is vulnerable to capture. An army must have arms, and it must have bread. Deprive it of either and, sooner or later, the fiercest fighters will be made to yield. Such was the case in Kars. Invaders didn't have to take this citadel. They had only to disrupt its supplies.

So many invaders: Seljuks and Byzantines, Georgians and Mongols, Turks and Russians. All bent on pillage and plunder; all with murder in their hearts. The blood they spilled, those invaders. So much blood. And for what? Some short-lived strategic advantage. Some short-term territorial gain. All reversed eventually. Pyrrhic victories. Blood spilled for nothing.

Down below, Kars looked small and densely packed. The plain wound around it, holding it in a kind of headlock. Perhaps the houses huddled as they did for comfort. One had to feel vulnerable in a place like this. It was noon now, and the faithful were being urged to pray. From up here, the chants sounded like howls. They put me in mind of those who had died on this frontier. Run through by steel or pierced by lead, this is how they would have sounded. What a terrible thing it is to end another's life.

I no longer much cared to see the citadel, but having had so much trouble getting there, I went in, anyway. I was glad I did. The fortress is a sham. Its thickset walls are mighty, and its wooden gates are grand. But step inside, and you're in a ruin. Every building in it has collapsed, the barracks and the mess halls and the store-rooms nothing more now than piles of tumbled stone.

A soldier stood guard in a grassy courtyard quite as big as a village common. No cottages or tea room, of course. No pubs offering a plowman's lunch. Just rubble. Even so, it would have made a perfect place for a game of cricket.

But it wasn't the courtyard that made me leave here whistling. It was that soldier. At the sight of me, he crossed his eyes and stabbed the air with his bayonet. He laughed when I affected fear. And then, just for the fun of it, he threw his head back and bayed like a lovelorn dog.

It was charming. Conscription, with its "dirty" food and "dirty" clothes, hadn't demoralized this man. And it gave me hope. Hope for Hussein, whose discontent had been weighing on me. It needn't have, I realized now, because Turks are skilled at making do. Hussein would survive his year and a half under arms. He had character.

———

Waiting to leave for Ani the next morning, I saw another altercation. This one involved two taxi drivers, one of whom accused the other of poaching his passengers. After trading threats, they dashed to their cars and returned, one with a tire iron, and the other with a screwdriver.

They were parted before they could harm each other. But unlike the melon incident, which, for all the noise it generated, had never seemed very dangerous, this one could easily have turned tragic. The claimants to the melon had *wanted* to be separated; not the taxi drivers. Had no one been there to stop them, one of these men might now be lying dead.

"I like Turks," said the man beside me. "But I wouldn't want to make one angry. They've vicious tempers."

A carpenter from Sydney, he and his wife—along with a couple from New Zealand—were going to Ani, too.

"Do you think so?" I said. "I find them rather gentle."

"They are," he said. "Up to a point. But get them going, and they'll stop at nothing."

Ani lies just thirty miles to the east of Kars, but the road is as rutted as corrugated tin, and it took us an hour and a half to get there.

"I see sheep, and I see mules," the carpenter said at one point. "Why don't I see any people?"

"I thought Armenians lived here," said his wife. "What happened to them?"

"Weren't they massacred?" said the man from New Zealand.

They were. In 1894. And again in 1915. As many as a million people. Turks, though, dispute the figure. People *did* die, they say, but not on any scale. There was no genocide.

Genocide or not, it was barbarous. Men were beheaded, women disemboweled, and children raped. People had their eyes put out and nails driven through their feet. They had their throats cut. They were burned alive. They were whipped and clubbed and left for dead. They were locked in cattle cars to die of hunger. They were hacked to pieces.

Armenians were rounded up by Turkish soldiers with chilling diligence. That Turkish tenacity again. I wonder about those soldiers. Were they also beaten by their officers? Did they dream of getting home? And how did they feel about the atrocities they committed? Like so many since, did they believe they were doing their duty?

In Europe, the Turk has long had a reputation for cruelty. For centuries, tales of Eastern barbarism proliferated: stories of young boys playing soccer with the heads of murdered Greeks; of watchmakers sawn in half for the crime of allowing a clock to stop; of women, suspected of infidelity, bundled into sacks and drowned at sea; of trained assassins deprived of their tongues to ensure their silence.

Were these stories true? It hardly mattered. Turkey had taken Bulgaria and Serbia and Hungary. And then it had set its sights on Vienna. As the sultan pushed west, he and his subjects became objects of fear. They weren't Western, and they weren't Christian, Europeans told themselves. They were savage and uncivilized. They were the Other.

Though not everyone agreed. For every Warburton who hated Turkey, there was a Burnaby who claimed to like it. Were the Turks such awful scoundrels? Burnaby crossed Turkey in 1876 for the purpose of finding out. "There was only one way to satisfy my own mind as to whether the subjects of the Porte were so cruel as they had been described," he wrote. "I determined to travel in Asia Minor.... Should I not behold Christians impaled and wriggling like worms on hooks in every high road of Armenia?"

In 1915, he would have seen just that. Not all Turks were to blame, of course. Many risked their lives to save Armenians. But in the West, it no longer mattered. Turkish savagery now became an idée fixe.

England denounced Turkey even though, some seventy years earlier, it had watched as famine killed a million Irish. And America denounced Turkey, forgetting that it had recently concluded its own war of annihilation—against its Indians.

It is not my intention to defend Turkey. But when we rail against its crimes, we should remember this: it isn't only Turks who excel at being cruel. There are Armenians in all our pasts.

"Look," said the carpenter. "There's Ani."

Before us on the rolling plain lay a ruined city high above a deep ravine and protected by a massive wall. That ravine, with its barbed wire and observation towers, marks the border between Turkey and what used to be the Soviet Union. Because it is deemed a restricted area by the army, no one is allowed to live there.

When kings ruled Armenia a thousand years ago, Ani was

their capital. Their reign was short—less than a century—and then, in 1045, control of Ani passed to the Byzantines. From the Byzantines, it passed to the Seljuks, and from them to the Georgians, and from them to the Kurds, and from them to the Mongols. No one ever held Ani for long. In 1319, there was an earthquake, and much of Ani was razed. No one has lived there since.

According to legend, Ani once boasted a thousand and one churches. Today, it has only seven—brown, crumbling shells that look like broken Easter eggs. They're small, these churches, and squat, and their roofs, what remain of them, are conical and set on high drums. The most impressive is the cathedral—a rectangle inscribed on a cross and embellished with pointed arches and blind arcades.

As lovely as the ruins are, what makes Ani special is its silence. It's not something you notice right away. When you arrive, it's the river you hear—that and the chatter of swallows. Ani is full of swallows, and they make a lot of noise. But sit quietly, and you notice something else. Something behind the chatter. You struggle to put a name to it—this thing you hear quite clearly now—and the only word that comes to mind is *silence*.

This can't be silence, you think. Silence is the *absence* of sound. And this is not like that at all. This "silence" is audible. A low, steady hum. Listening to it, I began to feel weightless. I had the sensation briefly that I was floating.

Ani is often described as holy. And I think that it has to be—despite the Soviet watchtowers just across the gorge. We talked a lot on the way there, the antipodeans and myself. But the moment we left the bus, all five of us fell instantly quiet. The place was obviously sacred—though none of us said as much—and something very deep in people responds to sacredness and wants to do it honor.

We walked around Ani not speaking a word. Then, one by

one, we slipped away. Five talkative people became four talkative people, then three, then two . . . The silence beckoned. It was something to enjoy alone.

I sat by a church and studied the swallows. A piece of rock broke loose and rattled into the gorge. I gazed down after it. Below me, a young boy, knee high in purple flowers, watched a black cow drink from the yellow river. And then the scene seemed to freeze. Nothing moved. Neither the boy nor the cow. Not even the rushing water. The world stood still.

It was a glorious day: the sky blue and cloudless, a sliver of moon, a light breeze, birdsong. And this enveloping quiet. So unlike Kars. Such a rowdy place, Kars. I felt so removed from it just then that I couldn't imagine ever having been there. Kars was another world. It was as far away as that sliver of moon.

I felt a surge of intense happiness. I'd liked Kars. Liked it enormously. But Ani was better. Here one knew what it means to be still.

chapter 6

To get to Doubayazit as quickly as possible, I would have to take "the dangerous route"—the road skirting the Iranian border and supposedly beset by smugglers and bandits.

The source of this information was a sixteen-year-old who worked for a bus company. He occupied a Naugahyde chair and wore horn-rimmed glasses. The chair was much too big for him, and so was his desk. And his typewriter. And his filing cabinet. It all seemed curiously out of scale, this office: massive furniture dwarfing a tiny magnate.

The bus company belonged to his father, who no longer took an interest in it.

"He's bought a hotel," said the teenager. "I run this place now."

He did so with huge aplomb. While we chatted, he took telephone calls and wrote tickets and drew up schedules and assigned duties and issued reprimands. He was never still.

It seemed a lot of responsibility for one so young, but not only did he relish it, he wanted more. He would study law when he left school, he said, and then he would stand for parliament.

"Perhaps you'll be president one day," I said, laughing.

"That's my intention," he said.

What would he do as head of state? I wanted to know. What would he change?

"Everything," he said. "By force, if I have to."

I asked him his name.

"Devrim," he said. "In English, it means revolution."

I inquired if the "dangerous route" to Doubayazit was *really* dangerous.

"You mean, will you be attacked?" he said. "It's possible. The long way is safer, but the buses are full until next week. Want to wait?"

I couldn't decide. The long way around might be less dangerous, but who would want it said of him that he shrank from taking risks? One was supposed to relish these dangers, to thrive on them. Travelers in the grand tradition cared nothing for their safety. They were the heirs of Richard Burton, who, crossing the Sinai, exulted in the knowledge that "the bursting of a water skin, or the pricking of a camel's hoof would be a certain death of torture."

"What can be more exciting?" he wanted to know, "what . . . more sublime?"

Why, nothing. Nothing at all. And yet . . . Those bandits. If anything like their forebears, they were certain to be nasty. Urquhart tells us of one ruffian who broiled his victims over red-hot coals and then sliced off their ears.

Even less pleasant were the female bandits who used to operate—and do so still, for all I know—not too far from Kars. After they had stripped their victim, a certain Major Millingen tells us in *Wild Life Amongst the Koords,* they performed "a series of dances . . . the object of which is to make the unfortunate victim lose his self-control. An attempt, however, on the part of the victim to reciprocate the advances of his alluring tyrants, becomes instantly fatal. The troop gets hold of him in a summary way . . . and condemn him to be pricked with thorns upon a very sensitive part of his person."

Unfortunate victims, indeed. But one can't help thinking they brought it on themselves. Certainly, it's hard to imagine Urquhart submitting to such treatment. According to Urquhart, you had to be firm with your captors. Show uncertainty, and you were lost.

Urquhart seems never to have known uncertainty. But then he had an advantage. He was English at a time when being English—to use the conventional phrase—"inspired respect." (Though if it inspired anything, it was more likely to have been fear.)

"I am English," Urquhart and his ilk would thunder, and the brigands threatening their lives would sheath their cutlasses and slink away. One didn't truck with English nationals. Too often, it caused a fuss.

Devrim was grinning at me.

"What's the matter?" he said. "Afraid?"

That did it! I summoned all my firmness.

"I'll take the dangerous route," I said.

"Are you sure?"

Burnaby had once been asked that very question. Was he sure he wanted to go to Khiva? It would be risky. "The Khan," he was told, "will very likely have your eyes taken out, or order you to be placed in the dungeon."

But the suggestion that he play it safe only made him bristle. (One imagines him raising that chin of his and squaring his massive shoulders.) Didn't the Russians realize that the English didn't shrink from danger? Others might turn tail. An Englishman stood his ground.

"I'm sure," I said.

The die was now cast, and I took my leave of Kars. I did so with some misgivings. I had liked it here. But in a way, that made leaving now all the more necessary. I should go before something happened to spoil it for me. That's one of the risks when you like a place: disillusionment.

Still, if you must be disappointed, sooner is better than later. Sooner, you've little invested in a place, so it hardly matters if it should fall short. Not later, though. That's when disappointment is especially cruel, tainting everything that went before, one unpleasant incident spoiling weeks of accumulated happiness.

The more time you spend in a place the more protective you become of this happiness, avoiding anything that might threaten it, eventually avoiding everything. You have but one aim now—to escape with your memories intact.

The road lurched and bumped across a dry watercourse and a line of sterile hills: the bare, forbidding landscape of eastern Anatolia. When it rains here and the grasses grow, this plain is beautiful. Not now, though. In mid-September, when all is a standard dun, it is stunning in its uniformity. And desolate, too. In three hours, I saw a single person—a bearded shepherd driving his flock to a watering hole.

From time to time, there were clusters of mud huts. Each hut had its own haystacks—forage for the winter—and its own fuel supply—bricks of dried dung arranged in pyramids. It would be an overstatement to describe these enclaves as villages. *Village* implies community, a suggestion of refinement. Here there was neither. The huts were long and low, their flat roofs made of sod. Gaze into them, and all one saw was blackness.

"It is strange how the mind can be amused amid scenery that presents so few objects to occupy it," Burton said once. But I found nothing to amuse me here. To avoid having to look at it, I read a novel.

The bandits can't have thought us of any great importance, because we arrived in Doubayazit in one piece and with our property intact. If only the touts had been half as discerning! They set upon us the moment we left the bus, pushing and shoving as they fought for our attention, shouting, pressing cards on us—for hotels, restaurants, travel agents—grabbing our bags, forcing us to grab them back again, grabbing our persons. They were, in short, a colossal nuisance. And there was no way to escape them. They had us surrounded.

It is a law of nature in much of Turkey: where tourists go, there go touts. Most offer a service of some sort—a better exchange rate, the name of a reputable guide, a discount at a carpet shop—for which they are paid a small commission. I'm sure they deserve it. But why, oh why, must they be so aggressive? These people inflict more discomfort than the ladies who jabbed their victims with thorns.

They're a shrewd lot. And accomplished. I admired especially their facility with languages. French? Italian? English? German? No trouble to them, they speak them all. (The smallest child in Doubayazit quoted prices in at least three tongues.) But much as you try to dwell on their qualities, you find yourself wishing they'd go away.

"Thank you," you tell them. "No hotel. I can find my own."

"No, I don't care to eat right now. I've just had lunch."

"The ruins? I think I'll sleep first, if you don't mind. Maybe tomorrow."

But still they press. So you start getting cross.

"Didn't you understand? I said no."

"No, no, no."

"Are you deaf or something?"

"I'm not going to repeat this: Sod off!"

The most dangerous touts, I discovered in Doubayazit, are the ones who look honest. Standing some distance from all this clamor (and looking as if he disapproved of it) was a young chap with one of those hairstyles that depend for their success on lots of mousse.

He smiled in my direction. An amused smile—detached, ironic, Augustan. I love smiles like that. I smiled back, and he waved me over. He knew of a hotel where a room with its own bath cost a mere six dollars. Was I interested?

I should have known better, I suppose. I should have told him to sod off, too. But how could I? He was smiling again.

"Lead the way," I said.

He led, and I followed. I followed for twenty minutes, at which point my legs began to tire.

"Is it much farther?" I asked.

"Five hundred meters."

So I followed him some more. Doubayazit is not large, I should explain, and we were traversing it for the second time when I spoke again.

"Just where *is* this place?" I suspected now that something was amiss.

"Just around the corner," I was told.

But it wasn't around the corner. Or the next corner. Or the corner after that.

"Didn't you say—"

He cut me short.

"We're just there."

Just there . . . almost there . . . nearly there. . . . We were getting closer all the time.

Just five more minutes now . . . three more minutes . . . two. . . .

And still we walked. And every time I wavered, some new amenity was introduced.

"Did I say you'll have your own phone?"

There was no one I knew in Doubayazit, so it wasn't likely

I would need a phone. But it had the desired effect. I steeled myself and soldiered on.

Later, when I seemed to weaken once again, I was told about the complimentary drinks.

"Your room has its own bar. You can drink all you want. It's free."

More walking. And then I put down my bag.

"I've had enough," I said. "I'm not taking another step."

"You don't have to," he said. "We're here."

From the outside, the hotel looked fairly comfortable. But there were no single rooms for six dollars, I was told at the desk. The cheapest single room cost three times that. And a bath, if I wanted one, could be had down the hall. I was livid. Really! This was no way to treat someone new to a place, someone who had just spent five hours on a smoke-filled bus.

"How do you explain this?" I said, wheeling on the tout. But he was no longer there. He was headed for the bus station, I expect, there to batten on someone else. I wished him luck. People as gullible as me didn't chance along too often.

I ended up finding my own hotel—a small, drab place up a crumbling flight of stairs. The shower was kept under lock and key and could only be used for a price. I've stayed in worse places, but after being tantalized with promises of telephones and liquor, it was something of a letdown. The owner, a surly fellow, refused to let me have a blanket. I wouldn't need one, he said. I didn't, as it happened. Still, it made me hopping mad.

Doubayazit is a shoddy little town with a bus station at one end and an open-air vegetable market at the other. Linking the two is the business district—an area of shops, banks, and offices lining a small grid of unpaved streets. Where the streets end, the houses begin—single-storied mud affairs, elongated and devoid of windows.

A truck sprayed water in an effort to keep the dust down—one more skirmish in a losing battle. After just an hour here, I had dust everywhere: in my eyes, in my nose, in my hair, in my ears. Few things are as intrusive as dust. When I spoke, it was dust I uttered. And when I listened, it was dust I heard. It was even in my mouth. I was ingesting dust. Bit by bit, it was filling me.

Most people who visit Doubayazit do so because they have to. Try to go anywhere in this part of Turkey—north, south, east, or west—and your route will take you through the center of town. Historically, people paused here to catch their breath—the dust permitting—and to reprovision. They do so still.

This is a Kurdish town and full of men in traditional Kurdish dress: flowing trousers, tight bomber jackets, a wide sash about the waist, and, on the head, a turban coiled like a wet towel. Kurds are wilder of countenance than Turks, more romantic looking. They have hooked noses and great shocks of long, black hair and dark eyes that stray past you when they speak to fix on something in the distance. They're a boisterous lot—intense and not always cordial.

While Turkey has ten million Kurds, officially it claims to have none. According to Ankara, these ten million aren't Kurds at all, but something it calls "mountain Turks." Long resigned to the futility of pressing for nationhood, most Kurds would now settle for cultural autonomy. But the government is opposed to even this. To make the Kurds assimilate, it has forbidden them to speak their own language, learn their own history, sing their own songs.

More and more, this repression is being resisted. For the past seven years, Turkey's army and members of the Kurdish Workers' Party have been locked in a guerrilla war that has claimed as many as three thousand lives.

I walked around Doubayazit three times in less than two hours. I decided not to stay very long. There were police and soldiers everywhere one looked. The young soldiers I'd seen in Kars had seemed fairly harmless. Here, with their rifles at the ready, they looked deadly. They were in Doubayazit to keep the peace, and if, to do so, they had to kill, one didn't doubt they would—without compunction. Doubayazit was an occupied town, however much the government denied it. There was even a policeman by the door of the billiard hall. Billiards? Seditious? When I tried to go in, he waved me away. An unsmiling fellow. Curious the impact of an unsmiling face in a country where most smile readily. It was almost chilling.

The day was winding down. Merchants stood in the doors of their shops and counted their takings. Unlike in Kars, here most shops closed at seven. By nine, the place was almost dead—though I did stumble on a video store. Inside, a soldier was renting *Karate Warrior*.

I was ready to turn in when a man came to the door of his shop and asked me in for tea. He introduced me to his two companions. One was a waiter and the other cut hair. I didn't like the look of the waiter. There was something sinister about him. He didn't once take his eyes off me.

At first, I tried not to notice. And when that didn't work, I told myself I was being overwrought. His interest was probably innocent. And then I glanced at him again. He was staring at my money belt.

So that was his game! The man was a bandit. Not the sort who swept out of hills on long-tailed ponies. The bandit, too, was much diminished, and this man was his modern descendant: the urban variety, the type who ambush their victims, not in lonely mountain passes but in darkened alleys. I patted my money belt. Good. It was firmly in place.

His associating with these other men made me think they were accomplices. It was dark now, and the town had fallen quiet. Was this their plan, then? To keep me here until everyone had gone indoors and then go through my pockets?

There was still no sign of the tea. The water was being boiled in an electric kettle, an antiquated thing, and it was taking an age. But every time I suggested leaving, my excuses were brushed aside. So we sat there, the four of us, not saying very much, and the starer saying nothing at all.

"Do you like being a waiter?" I asked him.

He shrugged his shoulders and waved a hand. Apparently, he spoke no English.

Ten more minutes passed, and still the water hadn't boiled. It struck me suddenly that it wasn't going to; that, in all likelihood, the kettle didn't work. It was a delaying tactic. I began to sweat. No one knew I was in this shop. Come to that, no one knew I was in Doubayazit. I wasn't registered with anyone. Not even the hotel. Normally, hotels ask to see your passport when you register. Mine hadn't. These men could cut my throat if they wanted to, and no one would ever know. I had to get out of here.

"Let me see if this kettle's working," I said. I stood up as if to cross the room and then made a bolt for the door. "Wait," someone shouted, but I paid no heed. I was in the street now, and I took to my heels. The hotel was almost a mile away. By the time I got there, I was gasping for breath.

I felt very tired the next day. Besides not having slept well, I was up at five to see Mount Ararat. Mighty Ararat, Burnaby called it, stretching "upwards into the realms of space, its lofty crest hidden in some vaporous clouds." Those clouds present a problem. Every day, a little after dawn, they descend to obscure the crest. To see *all* of Ararat, one has to get up early. I wasn't early enough. The clouds beat me to it.

"What a shame," said a man. "You came all this way for nothing."

It's wiser to travel without a specific object. Do otherwise, and you're courting disappointment. Too much can go wrong when you have an agenda. Besides, agendas are much too strenuous. The best way to travel is with no goals at all. The best travel is the sort you invent for yourself.

That's why I avoid "sights." Sights don't move me. To be moved, one has to be surprised, and by now the sights are too familiar. They've become too grand. All that admiration has gone to their heads. They expect to be liked now. They even insist on it. Attention in such quantity has made them vain.

I liked Ararat, what little I saw of it. At 17,000 feet, it is Turkey's highest peak, its snow-covered cone beckoning for miles. But even more than Ararat, I liked Tunga, the unkempt twelve-year-old I met coming back. A child of enormous self-assurance, he was disappointed, he said, that my Turkish would be so bad.

"Within ten years, Turkish will be a world language," he assured me.

Like those of so many Turkish children, his forehead seemed to bulge, an effect created by their skinhead haircuts. The intention is to discourage lice.

He opened the sack he carried to reveal a turkey, which, after looking me over, retracted its neck and withdrew from view.

Tunga said I could photograph this bird if I cared to—provided I paid a modeling fee. But turkeys hold no great interest for me, so I suggested, instead, that he join me for breakfast. Tunga thought for a moment, spat through a gap in his teeth, and accepted my invitation.

"Do you have children?" inquired this solemn little fellow with the poise of an adult. "I know. I shouldn't ask. Turks like children too much. One man I know has forty-four."

"That seems rather a lot," I said.

"I agree. Thirty is more than enough."

He took me to a windowless hovel where some twenty people—all men—sat at long tables and ate a meal of stale bread and lentil soup. It was still dark in there. I had to peer to see them. They sat hunched, their wizened faces not an inch from their bowls, and they ate without speaking a word. It was all very Trappist: the silence, the modest fare, the spartan conditions. When an old man entered, the waiter rushed to the door and kissed his hands. The ancient kissed the waiter on the eyelids.

Halfway through his soup, Tunga had a coughing fit.

"Excuse me," he said when he'd recovered himself. "I smoke too much."

He handed me what looked like a piece of glass.

"What is it?" I said.

"Obsidian. Take it. It's a present. Have you been to Ishak Pasha?"

"The citadel? No. I can't seem to find it."

"It's a few miles outside town. I'll take you if you give me a pack of cigarettes."

"I can't do that. Cigarettes are bad for you."

"Then give me your pen."

"Sorry. It's the only one I've got. Do you want the obsidian back?"

No, I could keep it, he said. But he'd changed his mind about the citadel. I'd have to find it myself.

And then he relented a little.

"It's a nice walk," he said. "I'll draw you a map."

On the way, I was set upon by four rapacious children. Dressed in tatters, they demanded money, and when I declined to give them any, they grabbed for my pockets. I had encountered the touts of tomorrow.

One of them, bolder than the others, managed to open my backpack, the others babbling while she worked. They were more than a match for me, and God knows what they might have done—stripped my bones, I shouldn't wonder—had an adult not chanced along and run them off.

In the last century, Dr. Karl Baedeker told his readers to affect "an air of calm indifference" when beset like this. And if indifference didn't work, they were advised to brandish a stick. At least one contemporary writer echoes this advice—though I can't see it having much effect. It would take an awful lot of brandishing to frighten *these* children. Besides, I don't think I'd care to threaten a child. And especially not a Turkish one. I admire them far too much.

There is a gravity about Turkish children that's quite enchanting. One doesn't expect such seriousness in the very young. Even their play seems subdued. And it's rare to see one make a fuss. Urquhart described them as having the manners of men. (Not *English*men, he was careful to stress. *They* had the manners of children.)

But is it so remarkable that Turkish boys would behave like men? After all, that's how many see themselves. Devrim, for example. And Tunga. And lots of others. In Turkey, the transition from child to adult is a gradual thing—not abrupt like it is in the West, and not nearly so traumatic. There is no flight from responsibility when a boy comes of age, because his whole life has been a training for manhood. Is this a loss to him as a child? Perhaps a small loss. But think how much he benefits when he's grown.

Turkish children are taught three things, a woman told me: to be self-reliant, to care for others, and to be satisfied with little. This last—the ability to make more of less—is the young Turk's special strength. In Kars, I saw two children amuse themselves with a drinking straw. For almost an hour they played. I hadn't realized it, but put your mind to it, and there are dozens of things one can do with a straw. Dozens.

When I arrived, the citadel appeared to be empty. A splendid square structure of honey-colored brick, it was built two hundred years ago by a local governor. He wanted it to be the most beautiful building in the world, he told his Armenian architect. And once it may have been. But the governor wasn't happy. What if the architect designed an even finer building for someone else? There was only one thing to do: he would amputate the Armenian's hands. According to legend, the architect died a pauper.

It's a ruin now, this yellow fortress with its yellow mosque and yellow minaret and yellow castellated keep. The courtyard is overgrown, and the halls are no longer marbled. But for all that, grandeur still clings to it. As fortresses go, this is still the beau ideal.

Built on a platform above a wide gorge and backed by jagged mountains, it overlooks what was once the Silk Route. No accident, this. The governor, something of a sybarite, financed his lavish life-style by exacting money from passing caravans. Back then, that sort of thing was looked on as banditry. Today, it is grandly referred to as "revenue enhancement."

I sat down and imagined the governor's agents charging from the citadel on long-maned horses. They wore fur caps, these men, and they had weathered faces, and their cries were the sort that curdle the blood. Their horses gathered speed, and the thunder of their hooves filled the gorge.

At the sight of this approaching horde, the terrified travelers urged on their mounts. But it was hopeless. Their animals were tired. They glanced back. The cutthroats were gaining on them. And what was more, they had drawn their sabers.

The travelers fled for cover. But there was little in a place like this. Just rock and bush. And soon the bandits were upon them, and the travelers dropped to their knees and pleaded for their lives.

The bandits want loot. And the travelers hand over everything they have—gold and lazuli, carpets and jade. All but one man, who hides a cherished watch in one of his saddlebags. The subterfuge is discovered, and there is an uproar.

Furious now, the bandits draw their sabers once again. The sun glints for one brief moment on all that steel. And then the miscreant is set upon, and his head rises off his shoulders. Rises. . . . Rises. . . . And now it starts to fall, rolling when it hits the ground, coming to a halt. The other travelers gaze down at it. It wears a look of utter puzzlement.

I heard a stone fall behind me and glanced around. And for a moment, I felt as those ancient travelers must have. There, not ten feet away, was the waiter! He had followed me here. Followed me *four miles*. There could be no doubting his intentions now. He clearly meant to do me harm.

He smiled. To put me at my ease, I suppose. But it didn't work. Some people are not good smilers, and he was one of them. Instead of making him look less sinister, this contraction of the facial muscles pulled his mouth into something of a leer.

Suppose he were armed. Damn it! I should have heeded Dr. Baedeker and brought a stick. I considered giving him my money. It wasn't all that much. Not enough to die for. Or maybe I should take the offensive. Surprise him by lunging at him. Yes, that seemed the better course. I'd give him a swift kick in the pants. That ought to bring him to his senses.

"What do you want?" I said, as I waited for a chance to rush him. And then I remembered he spoke no English. But I was wrong. He did.

"I need your help," he said. He sounded apprehensive. And it struck me then that he was frightened, too. Curious, isn't it, how quickly a perception can change. A moment ago, I thought he meant to murder me. Now I felt sorry for him.

"What kind of help?"

"My sister has been arrested."

"Well?"

"I want you to talk to the police. Ask them to let her go."

He glanced behind him. Did he think that someone had followed him as he had followed me?

"What was she arrested for?"

She was a university student, he said. Three months ago, a friend of hers had been arrested, and when she went to find out why, the police had locked her up. They had held her ever since. No charges had been laid against her.

"Can they do that?"

"They can do anything they want. But if you say you're a friend, they'll let her go."

"Why would that help? Why don't *you* talk to them?"

"I'm a Kurd," he said. "The police won't listen to me. They'll listen to you."

"Why?"

"You're a foreigner."

"Exactly. A stranger. I don't have any influence."

"Please."

"Listen, my involvement would only make things worse. The police would resent it."

"Please," he said again. He sounded stricken. He *looked* stricken. Though it may just have been his suit that made me think so. It was much too big. It made him look as if he might be shrinking.

"Why didn't you mention this last night?"

"I couldn't. One of those men is an informer."

"Have you discussed this with your sister?"

He shook his head.

"OK. I'll tell you what I'll do. I'll talk to your sister. And then I'll talk to the police—but only if she thinks it's a good idea."

She was being held in a small town north of Doubayazit, he said. There wasn't time to go there now. It was late afternoon. We arranged to meet the next morning. At my hotel.

"Nine o'clock," I said.

"Nine," he repeated. "I'll be there."

He didn't come at nine. I waited for hours, but he didn't come at all. At five that afternoon, I stopped waiting.

He's changed his mind, I thought. He's decided I was right; my involvement *would* complicate things.

I bought a ticket and left for Van.

———

The trip, through low, brown hills, would have been uneventful if the bus hadn't broken down. Just as the sun set, the engine failed. Engines, of course, are wont to fail. Which is why I have trouble liking them. They're much too unpredictable. They seem reliable—to start with, anyway—but they all break down eventually. It is a breach of faith—one that I, personally, find hard to forgive.

Turks are resourceful when it comes to making stopgap repairs. But this engine was beyond the resources not only of our driver, but of all twelve passengers, each of whom had his own ideas as to what the problem was and how it might be remedied. We'd have to wait for another bus to chance along.

"How long do you think we'll be here?" I asked the driver.

"Maybe until morning," he said. "Unless bandits find us first."

"Is that likely?"

He shrugged. "Who knows?"

A bus *did* pick us up just before dawn, but I have to tell you, it was a miserable night. It wasn't being hungry that I minded. Or the man beside me fondling my knee and winking furiously. Worse than that—worse than anything—was the general unease. The people on this bus were frightened. You didn't know with bandits, they said. Sometimes they killed; sometimes they didn't.

Had any of them ever been attacked? I asked.

No, they said. They hadn't.

Their friends, then?

No, not friends, either. But friends of friends. They had all heard stories: tales of people being robbed and beaten, or left for dead, or abducted—whisked into the hills and never seen again.

In no time, I was frightened, too. I was ashamed of myself for yielding so easily. It was something Urquhart would not have done. Or Burnaby. Or Warburton. And compounding my shame was guilt. I should have stayed in Doubayazit. I should have looked for the waiter. I should have tried to help his sister.

There was no avoiding it. I was not in the heroic mold. Unlike Burton, who left home to show his mettle—and show it he would, even if it killed him—I had left home with the firm intention of returning.

I don't mind discomfort. Faced with discomfort, one simply hunkers down. I don't mind hardship, either. Hardship is good for a man. Smollett suffered much at the hands of the French, but because of it, he returned to England cured of his bad temper. No, hardship can be borne—as long as it isn't life-threatening. I'm averse to placing myself in mortal danger. I simply refuse to risk my life.

I am no Wolff. Wolff was impervious to danger. Crossing Asia, he was shot at, poisoned, and incarcerated. He survived an attempt to burn him alive. He was attacked by swarms of bees. Buildings fell on him. He almost drowned. He was tied to the tail of a horse and dragged through scrub. He came down with dysentery and cholera. But his greatest feat was crossing the Hindu Kush after bandits had stolen his clothes. To take his mind off the cold, he recited Goethe.

This chronicle of disasters has something preposterous about it, something worthy of Baron von Münchhausen. But in Wolff's case, the stories were true. Outlandish people lead outlandish lives, and Wolff is proof. His narrow escapes were legion—so many that one is tempted to wonder if he didn't, as he himself claimed, enjoy special protection.

But even more remarkable is that, for all his close shaves, Wolff never once became discouraged. Another man would have wavered, cut his losses and turned for home. Not Wolff. He didn't so much as complain. He had to have been an astonishing person.

chapter 7

God Almighty! The surprise—the shock, even—of coming upon Lake Van!

All day, we'd rumbled across yet more of the barren Anatolian plateau, so familiar now I barely noticed it. I no longer expected water. I had forgotten what it looked like. And then the road turned suddenly, and there it was: this huge basin measuring over 1,400 square miles—six times the size of Lake Geneva. More water than I'd seen in weeks. Far away it stretched. As far as the horizon. Enough water, it seemed, to drown a dozen Anatolias. It took the breath away.

It must be allowed, of course, that one's first glimpse of any stretch of water is a special moment. Even stolid Burnaby was uncharacteristically moved when he first laid eyes on "the mighty Oxus."

"I gazed on that world-renowned stream," he wrote, "which, in my boyish days, it had been my dream to visit."

It could sometimes happen that one's boyish dreams were dashed. "I own I am greatly disappointed by the Euphrates," wrote James Fraser, and the words strike home because Fraser was a man who resisted disappointment. But occasions like that were rare. A more typical reaction was that of Kinglake, who, seeing the Marmara for the first time—the "mighty Marmara" others have called it—became so enchanted that nothing would suffice but to "plunge into its depths and quench my longing love in the palpable waves."

The "mighty" Oxus; the "mighty" Marmara. Travel writers don't hesitate to describe rivers and seas as "mighty." And their size has little to do with it. The "mighty" Aegean and the "mighty" Congo are all well and good. But the "mighty" Seine? The "mighty" Thames?

No one would deny that oceans are mighty, but here, for some reason, writers are more equivocal. Oscar Wilde thought the Atlantic not mighty enough—"It is not so majestic as I expected," he said—while another writer, the Marchioness of Dufferin and Ava, faulted the Pacific for being *too* mighty. It was, she complained, downright nasty.

"A horrid pot of blue paint," Walter Pater called one of the lakes of Switzerland. Not Lake Van. It's far too big to be a pot. It's more a giant caldron. And it isn't blue at all. It's gray—even when the sun is shining. This is something its composition may explain. The lake is highly alkaline, which means apparently— and this is only hearsay—that one can wash in these waters without benefit of soap.

I found this information in a guidebook. Actually, I found it in several guidebooks. It is one of those details that guidebooks seize on, supposing them, I imagine, to provide what is known as "color." Color needn't be new. Which is just as well, because it rarely is. Read these books, and what one notices is this: the same color crops up in most of them.

Neither, for that matter, need color be true. The cherry is a case in point. The cherry, one reads repeatedly, originated in Giresun, where it was noticed by Lucullus, who had the idea of taking it back to Italy. But would he have bothered? I hardly think so. Italy, after all, already had cherries. Quite a lot of them.

Something reminiscent of Evelyn Waugh's *Scoop* may be at work here. A story deemed "true" by virtue of having appeared in *one* book now appears in others, convincing the creator that he can't really have made it up because, if he had, someone would surely have said so.

At first sight, the town of Van looked delightful. "An air of comfort reigned about," and after the rigors of Doubayazit, one had the feeling of entering a great metropolis. The boulevards were wide and lined with trees, and the shops were new and crammed with delicacies. Smartly dressed people filled the sidewalks, cars filled the streets, diners filled the restaurants, and happiness filled my heart. I was back in civilization.

Which meant I had better shape up. I was looking like Robinson Crusoe, and this wouldn't do at all. Not in cosmopolitan Van. I took a shower and washed my hair. I shaved. I cut my fingernails. I clipped my mustache. I cut my toenails. I filed the calluses on my feet. I polished my shoes. And, finally, I changed my clothes.

I stepped in front of the mirror. There was no marked improvement that I could see, but at least I was clean.

I planned to spend a week in Van, so I did some washing: jeans, T-shirts, and what the Victorians referred to as their "unmentionables." Clothes hung in hotel rooms can take days to dry. That's why laundering, like agriculture, demands a measure of stability. This is something anthropologists might investigate: does the hygiene of hunter-gatherers improve when they settle down? I'll wager anything it does.

I went downstairs and ate a delicious dinner: lamb stew with saffron rice and just-baked bread. Afterwards, I had coffee. And a cake—one of those currant things I'd live on given half the chance. And a bar of chocolate. Nature's bounty, chocolate. All the nutrients allowed by law. Ah, the pleasures of the flesh. But all that dissipation wore me out. After struggling up to bed, I slept more soundly than I had in weeks.

Seen in the light of day the next morning, Van proved less grand than I had thought it. It was a Potemkin village of a place. The shops I had so admired—the ones that brimmed with delicacies—did, indeed, line a wide boulevard. But stray from this thoroughfare and, immediately, one was back in Asia. No delicacies now. No smartly dressed crowds. Just narrow, twisting streets. And fruit barrows. And market stalls. And taxis. And horse-drawn carts. And craftsmen working in tiny shops. And noise. So much noise. It was deafening. And irresistible.

The pavements were spread with pottery and engine parts and shoes and portable radios. Two carts collided, and several hundred eggs fell to the ground. A shopkeeper, a dagger in his belt, cursed a man who had dropped a vase. Two dogs fought for possession of an apple. A child darted between my legs and almost bowled me over. Everyone here was male. Even those shopping for children's clothes.

I turned a corner and found myself in the meat market. A covered alley, it was dark and stifling and smelled of rot. Blood everywhere. Carcasses swaying on meat hooks. Bowls of sheep's eyes. Animal parts and intestines strewn about the ground or piled on tabletops. It was a charnel house. And the air so vile, I could hardly breathe.

Outside again, I watched several small boys play a game of soccer in the street. Their efforts were complicated by a steady stream of traffic. But the boys were fearless, leaping into the path of cars and, just as quickly, leaping out again. It must have been hair-raising for the drivers, but only once did I see one lose his composure. It happened when the ball landed on his car and splattered it with mud.

"Who did that?" the driver shouted. And when the culprit

was pointed out to him, he leaned out the window and directed a well-aimed spit at the miscreant's head.

Later, the ball landed at my feet, and I discovered it was not a ball at all. It was the head of something. The head of a sheep.

I walked a block and was back on Van's main boulevard. Two worlds side by side. Past and present contiguous. Touching, but—and this was the odd part—not appearing to alter each other. They simply coexisted.

There were no broken eggs on this boulevard, no animal parts, no squabbling dogs. Just this lackluster modernity. It seemed so inanimate now. So lifeless. Ten minutes of it was enough, and I was heading back. Back to the carts and barrows. Back to the twisting streets. Who cared about the charnel house or the head doing service as a ball? The place was vivid. It was alive.

————

I ended up being thankful for Van's pretensions because, without them, it isn't likely I'd have found my Marmite. I had been craving Marmite, a yeast extract and a staple of the British diet, for several weeks, and now—in one of those shops that cater to the needs of visitors—there it was: a large black jar with a yellow label bearing in red letters the magic word: M-A-R-M-I-T-E. What happiness!

An interesting shop, it sold not only Marmite, but Ovaltine, and Chivers marmalade, and Cadbury's chocolate, and Typhoo tea, and Jacob's cream crackers, and Bird's custard, and so much else of English manufacture that it might have been one of Harrods' food halls.

The chap inside, a fellow in his late twenties, looked surprised when I told him what I wanted.

"Are you sure?" he said, blowing the dust off it. "It's been here awhile."

I said I was quite sure.

"Have you tasted it?" he wanted to know. "It's awful."

I told him that I had tasted it and didn't find it awful at all. At which point, he consented to let me have it.

"How much?" I said.

"Does thirty thousand lira seem a lot?"

I said it did.

"Ten thousand?"

The shop was his father's, he said. He himself had just returned to Van after ten years in Germany. Five of those years had been spent in jail.

"What for?"

"You know those bank machines with money in them? I tired to break into one."

"What was prison like?"

"Great," he said with much enthusiasm. "We had videos, billiards, *Playboy*. I loved it."

He now hoped to go to England, having no doubt heard that it, too, had bank machines. He inquired if the English authorities would know about his record.

"It's possible," I said. "Interpol."

"Maybe I can bribe someone."

"I'm not sure that's such a good idea. Bribes never really caught on in England."

He said this surprised him. He had thought England a civilized country, and he wondered now if he shouldn't go to America, instead.

"I'm a bodybuilder. Maybe I'll go to New York and become Mr. Universe."

His name was Ahmet, and if his plans were a little grandiose, it didn't diminish his charm. His hair, tightly curled, extended below his shoulders and made him look like a King Charles spaniel. He loved Europe, he said, and he longed to return there.

"I was born in Turkey," he said, "but in my heart, I'm a European. I like European clothes and European women and European food. Do you like the Rolling Stones?"

"Yes. And you?"

"Of course. Their music is modern. Not like Turkish music. I listen to them all the time."

As there were Turks who wanted to be Europeans, so were there Europeans who wanted to be Turks. I met one of the latter at breakfast the next morning. His name was Peter, and he was Dutch—though you would never have known it to see him. He wore voluminous trousers and a turban, the ends of which dangled about his ears. A sash completed the effect—or would have had it not kept falling off. Peter was as thin as Gandhi.

His breakfast was a piece of bread and a glass of tea. My own repast was more elaborate—stuffed green peppers, grilled meatballs, and an onion salad. To ease my embarrassment, I pretended I'd been sick.

"I don't normally eat this much," I said. "This is my first meal in a week."

At the mention of illness, he drew back.

"Nothing serious, was it?" he said. "I must be careful. I'm not very strong."

Small wonder. He hardly ate at all. During the three days we spent together, he lived on a diet of bread and yoghurt. He reminded me of St. John the Baptist, who was said to have existed on just locusts and honey.

Peter had last worked twelve years ago, surviving since on a small stipend provided monthly by the Dutch government. Every other week, he telephoned to Holland in case the authorities might have found him a job. So far, they hadn't.

Not that Peter cared. If he had his way, he said, he'd never work again.

Then he didn't mind living at the expense of others?

But he wasn't, he said. People don't produce wealth anymore. Machines do. If I were asking then, if he minded existing at the expense of *machines,* the answer was no, he didn't. Could I think of a reason why he should?

He liked to hold forth on the evils of industrial society. It had defiled the planet and made all of us less human. Europe was a spent force. It had lost its moral authority. It no longer had a soul.

I didn't doubt his sincerity and was, besides, as concerned about Europe's soul as he was. But all of this rankled, somehow. Certainly, industrial society did test one's decency. Tested it rather too much. But one met the test. Or tried to, anyway. One didn't run away. Not because running away wasn't loyal, but because it didn't gain one anything. The moral challenges facing one in Europe were the same challenges one faced in Turkey and Zambia and Costa Rica and anywhere else people tried to be decent. And donning a turban didn't make a whit of difference. Becoming virtuous entailed something more than a change of headwear.

Warburton, great stickler for form that he was, would not have liked Peter. Peter had gone native. He had violated one of Warburton's cardinal rules. "It is too frequently the habit among [Europeans] to dress ludicrously or meanly," he wrote. "This is a great mistake, and militates much against the wearer. In the East, dress is naturally looked upon as a test of the wearer's quality; and he cannot be surprised if he is treated accordingly."

Nor would Warburton have liked Mansfield Parkyns, who, for three years in Abyssinia, wore nothing but a short kilt of antelope hide and the skin of a jackal. His behavior during those three years, said Lady Palmerston, who met him in London, represented "the most successful attempt by a man to reduce himself to the savage state."

Did going native, this zeal for local values, suggest weakness of character? Very often, that was how it was seen. Parkyns was accused not only of making a show of himself, but of disgracing his class and—even worse—of shaming England. He had, it was generally agreed, "let the side down."

He paid dearly for his enthusiasms. Reviewing Parkyns's book in *Blackwood's,* Frederick Hardman described the writer as "an amateur barbarian."

"Fancy," he told his readers, "a civilized Englishman, pitching his tent for three years amongst filthy savages . . . eating raw beef . . . and upon his return home, coolly publishing his confessions . . . as if he would say, See what a fine fellow I am to have thus converted myself into a greasy, shoeless savage."

It was all a little harsh. Parkyns was the gentlest of people and an admirable man. What seems to have inflamed his critics was his refusal to browbeat people. Unlike Warburton, who advised travelers to "insist on the most profound respect," Parkyns relied on "a civil tongue and a quiet unpretending manner." Arriving in a village, he wrote, "I have always found it a better plan to wait under a tree till someone asks me in."

Parkyns, who saw civilization as something of a nuisance, spoke often of "the excitement of a savage life." He lived simply, his only possessions "a kid-skin filled with flour, a little horn of cayenne pepper . . . and a small piece of thin leather for a bed." He said they were all he needed. Back in England, a country in which he never felt at home, he declared his years in Abyssinia—years of "peace and innocence," he called them—to be the happiest of his life.

Because Parkyns was the kind of traveler I'd want to be myself, I began to take a kinder view of Peter, seeing his wardrobe as not so much a lack of character as an attempt to enter fully into another culture. Peter was trying to lose himself, and I could hardly despise him for it. By pursuing the exotic, I was attempting much the same.

———

Ahmet might have been a European, as he said, in his heart, but he had much to learn about European punctuality. He wanted to show me Van's museum and had named a tea shop in which we were to meet one afternoon. "I'll be there at three," he said. "On the dot."

The dot came and went, but there was no Ahmet. Three fifteen. . . . Three thirty. . . . There was still no sign of him, and I pondered what to do. Stand on my dignity, as Warburton would have, and leave in high dudgeon? Or adopt "a quiet unpretending manner" like Mansfield Parkyns, and wait without making a fuss?

I decided to wait. I wanted an hour. And a most uncomfortable hour it proved to be. Everyone here wanted to talk to me. I had become an object of intense interest.

First, I was approached by a succession of bootblacks, and after that by a succession of taxi drivers. Then it was the turn of students anxious to practice their English—one wanted help with the subjunctive, something I know nothing about—and after them came the fragrance sellers, one of whom sprayed my hand with something that smelled like oven cleaner.

Quite a pleasant smell, really, evoking as it did hearth and home. There are those, perhaps, who wouldn't care to smell of oven cleaner, but I rather liked the idea. It had all the right connotations: *Kinder, Kirche, Küche.*

Ahmet turned up, finally, and rescued me, but it was only a partial rescue because, before going to the museum, he wanted me to meet a friend of his—a carpet seller.

"I don't want a carpet," I said.

"This isn't business," he said. "It's a social call."

But it was nothing of the sort. Ahmet's friend was a small man with protruding ears, and I could feel his interest quicken when I crossed his threshold. A customer, by God! I declined his offer of tea, not wanting to feel obligated. But my protestations were ignored, and it was sent for anyway. And then, inevitably, the rugs were produced.

"I'm not interested," I said. "And besides, I don't have any money."

"I know," said the friend. "I just want you to see them."

"OK," I said.

I didn't want to appear rude. But that was a mistake because, frankly, where carpet sellers are concerned, nothing short of rudeness has the least effect.

The friend nodded gravely, giving me to think that we had an understanding. But had we? A minute later, he wanted to know how much I meant to spend. I appealed to Ahmet. "Please tell him I have nothing." But Ahmet, whose Turkish loyalties ran deeper than he realized, only shrugged. This was a matter for me and his countryman. He had no intention of getting involved.

I had no choice but to cut this short.

"I'm sorry," I said, getting up to leave. "There's been a misunderstanding."

But the friend wouldn't hear of my going.

"Sit down, sit down," he said. "If you don't want a carpet, you don't want a carpet."

More tea was sent for, and the conversation turned to other things. But not for long. Soon, carpets came up again—their investment value this time—and rugs were being thrown to the floor in front of me like cards from a giant deck.

"You like them?"

"I like them, but I don't want them," I said, my voice rising. The Warburton in me was coming out again. It might have been simpler to say I *didn't* like them. But that would have been untrue. And anyway, he would have found that no more credible than my claiming to have no money. As he saw it, it was all a bargaining strategy, this professed lack of interest. It was all a ploy.

Now he raised the subject of shipping arrangements.

"No shipping," I said.

"You'll take it with you?"

I'm not very good in these situations. I'm fine with reasonable people and have even had some success with *un*reasonable ones. What I can't handle are unreasonable people who *appear* reasonable. That sort of thing unnerves me completely. I wasn't getting through to this man. Why? Was that his fault or was it mine? How had I failed to make myself clear? What did I have to do? I mean, I'd been quite categorical. "No," I had said. "No." "No." "No." But what I meant when I said "no" was not what he thought I meant. And when he said, "I understand," he didn't mean "I understand what you're saying." He meant "I understand what you're *doing*." When, actually, he only thought he did. We had taken the same words and invested them with different values. We were doomed to mutual incomprehension.

I should know better, I suppose, but I prize words. I think they should be used with care because misuse them, and they're diminished. I think people should mean what they say, and that's not possible when words are treated lightly. I think people should be honest—impossible if the words we use serve only to mislead. I think words should illuminate, not obscure. Without a language that is clear and unambiguous, there's just no point in our talking to one another.

"I have to go now," I said. "Good-bye."

Ahmet followed me out. I thought he would apologize, this

man with a European heart, but he said nothing. It was I who spoke first.

"I have nowhere to put a carpet," I said. "I have a small apartment."

"Don't you have walls?" he asked.

"Yes. Why?"

"You could hang a carpet there."

If Ahmet wasn't all he seemed, neither, for that matter, was Peter. Needing an aspirin, I went to his room one night and found him, still in his turban, listening to Beethoven on a cassette player.

"So you haven't rejected Western civilization entirely," I said.

"Not completely," he said, grinning. "It can boast its achievements."

"And Turkish music?"

He pulled a face.

"Can't stand it," he said.

Peter was traveling with all nine of Beethoven's symphonies, four of Bach's Brandenburg Concerti, twenty Chopin études, sixteen string quartets by Mozart, and much of *La Traviata*. All in all, it was a sizable collection.

"It can't be easy carting it about," I said.

"It's worth it," he said. "This is how I get my consolation."

I got *my* consolation from a volume of Shelley's poems. Traveling is great fun, but once in a while, it overwhelms one. For a brief time, abroad becomes *too* abroad, and one turns to some familiar object to mitigate the foreignness of it all.

As such objects went, Peter's tapes were hardly excessive. Smollett arrived in Boulogne in 1763 with a library that included the works of Homer, Sophocles, and Virgil, and more than a hundred volumes he had penned himself. (Though so busy was he finding fault with France, one doubts he found much time for reading.)

Twelve years later, Captain Philip Thicknesse sailed for the continent with two guitars, a violin, a cello, a parakeet, and a monkey whose derby had been made by a leading London hatter. (The parakeet was not to make it back alive. In Calais, the hapless bird was eaten by a dog.)

Pietro della Valle derived *his* consolation—and grim it must have been—from the decomposing body of Maani, his wife. She had died when she and her husband were visiting the Middle East, but instead of burying her, he preferred to keep her with him, and together they visited Persia and India. Maani can't have been much of a traveling companion. When finally buried in 1626, "her head [was] wasted away and without flesh."

People rarely travel with cadavers anymore. Rarely travel with extensive libraries. Travel nowadays with a corpse or the works of Dickens and you must carry them yourself. Not so in the past. Then there were retinues. Wonderful things, retinues. To smooth your path and ensure your comfort, there was nothing they mightn't do. Thackeray didn't actually *climb* the Great Pyramid. He was carried to the top by four Arabs engaged for that very purpose.

Retinues could sometimes be large. Walter Plowden, whom Mansfield Parkyns met in Egypt, had so much luggage, it took eight porters to carry it. Benjamin Disraeli's entourage was even bigger. The future prime minister crossed Albania in 1830 with two guards, six Turkish guides, a translator, and a gazelle. The gazelle was nice to look at, said Disraeli, "but [he] gave us a great deal of trouble."

Not everyone, though, cared to travel with servants. When Burnaby went to Khiva, he went alone. Servants, he complained, "are generally in the way."

They also needed discipline, and not everyone felt up to providing it. Not Burnaby, of course. Where Burnaby was concerned, justice was invariably swift. When a careless Russian driver tipped him and his luggage into a snowdrift, "I resolved to appeal to his feelings by a sharp application of my boot."

"You hurt, you break my ribs," the driver protested.

It was a cowardly thing to do, and it quite ruined the book for me. After that, all of Burnaby's sangfroid rang hollow. The man was a common bully.

In the old days, even those travelers who didn't want one could afford a servant. If they chose to, they might have several. Servants were cheap. Travel was cheap.

"About fifty pounds a month covers all the expenses that the traveller, unless very luxurious, can require in the East," wrote Warburton in 1845. That's twenty-five dollars a *week* for "first-class accommodations, provisions and wine *a discretion.*"

I, not in the least luxurious, was spending twenty-five dollars a day. My hotel accounted for a third of that. As for the rest, I've no idea where it went. I didn't buy anything, and I wasn't spending it on meals. (After a week of gluttony, my puritan side was in the ascendant again, and like Peter, all I ate was bread and yoghurt.) In some way I never quite determined, my money dwindled to nothing, and I would find myself cashing one more traveler's check.

Cashing a check in Van proved something of a trial, albeit an amusing one. The bank I went to *looked* modern. Behind a gleaming plate-glass window, people sat at gleaming computer terminals and pored over spreadsheets. But how modern was it *actually*? In Van, *looking* modern and *being* modern were not to be confused.

Everyone was working feverishly when I went in, so feverishly I wasn't noticed. I cleared my throat, and one person did glance up, but it can't have been the right person, because she promptly glanced down again, so I cleared my throat once more. This time another person glanced up, but he can't have been the right person, either. Just as quickly, he glanced down, too.

I cleared my throat again, and this time no one glanced up. If anything, they now seemed busier than ever. Some clutched phones and talked, while others clutched phones and stared into space. These latter I took to be holding for someone because they rolled their eyes a lot. One was to believe, I think, that their patience was being tried.

The woman at the desk nearest me was rolling her eyes with particular vigor, so I said, simply by way of conversation, "Isn't it maddening being made to wait?"

I meant it was maddening for her, but she misunderstood and took me to mean maddening for *me*. Which didn't please her at all. My reward for this conversational gambit was a glare.

"Did you want something?" she asked icily.

"Well, yes. I hoped to cash a traveler's check."

"The foreign-exchange department is upstairs," she said, no longer looking at me. She was staring into space again.

The attractive woman in foreign exchange pleaded ignorance when I showed her my check. What was it for? she wanted to know. I explained as well as I could, but she now professed to be even more confused. My fault entirely. My knowledge of banking is shaky at best.

"Wait," she said. "I'll have to get my supervisor."

Her supervisor, another attractive woman, understood about traveler's checks, so that wasn't a problem. What she didn't understand, she said, was how I came to have one. I explained that I'd bought it—along with several others—in New York. But this only made her more suspicious. She wanted to know how many I had in all. And then she asked to see them.

She rubbed a finger across each check—to establish, I suppose, that the ink was dry—and while she did so, a security guard placed himself conspicuously at the top of the stairs in case I should panic and try to bolt.

The rubbing completed, the woman checked the numbers against a list she took from a drawer. It was a long process and, while she worked, I thought of Burnaby in Orenburg, where a cashier "did not look with much respect upon Coutts' circular notes, or upon a letter of credit from Cox and Co., the well-known bankers. . . . When I told him that the paper of these two English bankers was looked upon in London as being as good as gold, the clerk shook his head, and evidently did not believe me."

(One wonders if a Russian presenting his circular notes in London would have fared much better.)

Finally, and with great reluctance, my checks were returned.

"They seem all right," said the supervisor. She sounded disappointed.

"Then you'll cash one?" I said.

"I'll have to see your passport."

I handed her my Irish passport and was promptly asked why it wouldn't be American.

"Why should it?"

"You said you bought your checks in New York."

"I *live* in New York."

"Without an American passport?"

"Yes."

"Isn't that unusual?"

"Not in the least."

Certain now of my criminal intent, she summoned two of her colleagues who were drinking tea and clearly resented this interruption. Page by page and with great concentration, they examined the passport. It was pored over, thumbed through, and passed from hand to hand. At one point, they held it by the covers and shook it. A new document when I gave it to them, it was returned to me looking old and worn.

"Is it in order, then?" I asked.

The three of them conferred and admitted that it was.

"But we can't cash your check now," said the supervisor.

"Why ever not?"

"Because it's four fifteen," she said. "We stop cashing checks at three thirty. You'll have to come back tomorrow."

My advice should you ever go to Van is this: carry coin, if that is what it takes. But whatever you do, and however much you might be tempted, *avoid the banks*!

chapter 8

The touts in Adiyaman were unusually aggressive, rounding us up like sheep when our bus arrived and herding us, against our will and over our protests, into a holding pen they called a tourist information office. When I showed signs of wandering off, I was pursued by a man in a fur-lined coat, who snapped and barked with all the vigor of a Border collie.

"You have to report to the office," he insisted. "It's a rule."

Mention of rules made me wonder if the place didn't serve an official function. Were we in a military zone? There were so many in Turkey, I couldn't remember.

"What's in there?" I asked him. There was something predatory about this man. His teeth protruded, and his nose twitched. What was he doing? Testing the air for the presence of prey?

"It's a rule," he said again. "You have to show your passport."

Nothing is more calming to the official mind than the sight of a passport—though just why is far from clear. A passport is thought to confer legitimacy, to attest to the bearer's good repute. But does it really? Almost anyone can have a passport—and those who can't may, with a little effort and at no great expense, have one forged.

A forged passport is better than a real one, I have always thought. The bearer of a bogus passport can be anyone he likes.

In Africa once, I met a man with *three* passports. "Who will I be today?" he would say when we neared a frontier. "A Pole? A Bulgarian? An East German?" Of all the people I have met, he is the one I envy most.

I didn't have to show my passport, as it happened. There was no one to whom I might have shown it. No one remotely official, that is. The only people in the tourist information office were *more* touts. And a clamorous lot they were. If those outside had suggested nothing so much as sheepdogs, those in here put one in mind of wolves. Outside, it had struck me that we might be fleeced. Now I had to wonder if they would bleed us dry as well.

I hate being badgered like this. It's unpleasant. It's a waste of one's time. And it's exhausting.

"I'm sorry," said our driver, who was clearly embarrassed. "They're a new generation. They're not us."

By "us" he meant older Turks—people reconciled to having little. The touts aren't like that. The touts have had their fill of being poor. They want to improve their lot. And that does them credit. Those who romanticize poverty can't ever have experienced it. Poverty is miserable, and the touts are right to want to escape it. But must they do so in quite this fashion?

After being rendered almost senseless by this barrage, we found ourselves—whether willingly or not, none of us could say—crowded into a minivan that would take us to Kahta.

There were five of us in all: myself; an Australian teacher and his doctor-wife; a German student; and a man from Holland, a nurse. We had teamed up in Van because we had a common purpose: to travel to Adiyaman and, from there, go to Nemrut Dagi to see the tomb-sanctuary of King Antiochus.

"Why Kahta?" said the doctor, who seemed even more bewildered than the rest of us.

"They said something about spending the night there," said

the student. Though not yet twenty, he was almost bald. "We'll go to Nemrut tomorrow."

We were about to pull away when the man in the fur-lined coat came hurrying towards us. Actually, he only seemed to hurry. When he walked, his right foot turned inward, making him appear to scuttle.

He had decided to accompany us to Kahta, he said. He had taken a liking to us. (Saying this, he winked in the direction of his comrades, who roared with laughter.) Yes, he said, once in a while, a group of tourists chanced along to whom he instantly warmed. He had no idea why.

"Do you know why?" he said, turning to his colleagues in mock appeal. But his confederates shook their heads. They could no more explain this phenomenon than he could. They were laughing so hard they couldn't speak.

"See?" he said. "They don't know, either. It's a mystery."

He squeezed into the front seat.

"I'm going to take a personal interest in you," he continued. "I think of you now as friends."

For a while, he behaved as if he meant it. Once we got going, he told us that Kahta had several good hotels.

"Which is the best?" said Sarah, the doctor. She was plump and soft and wore a purple smock. She reminded one of a ripe eggplant.

"I'm going to show you all of them," he said. "You can decide for yourself."

But after that, he became less and less communicative. When the student inquired if his coat wasn't very hot, his answer was a snarl.

"He must have made a mistake," said Ted, the teacher, a short man who fretted about his height. "He doesn't like us, after all."

Clearly, he didn't because, in Kahta, instead of the hotels we were promised, he dropped us in front of a small pension. And when we complained, he tossed our bags into the street. Then the bus drove off. We were stranded.

"What an unpleasant man," said Sarah.

Ted, her husband, was more explicit. "He's more than unpleasant," he said. "He's a prick."

We had two choices: stay put or, laden with bags, walk into town. The pension left much to be desired—it boasted eight showers and eight toilets, but of the former, only one worked and, of the latter, none at all. But the walk into town promised to be a long one. So, far from happy and cursing the man in the fur-lined coat, we elected to stay.

We hadn't seen the last of this fellow. An hour later, he reappeared and, going from room to room, told us to assemble for a sales pitch.

It would have to wait, we said; we'd had our fill of sales pitches. And besides, we'd been traveling for sixteen hours. We were tired.

But the man in the coat was adamant. He was going downstairs, he said. He would expect us in five minutes. Earlier just sullen, now he was openly hostile.

Warburton would never have tolerated such behavior and, after a great deal of muttering, it was decided that we wouldn't, either. The man was a bully, we agreed, and someone would have to tell him.

"But who?" I said. It was certainly not a job *I'd* want. But my speaking only drew attention to me, and Sarah said, "Why not *you*?" and before I could object, the student said, "The very man," and then everyone was nodding, and Benny, the nurse, slapped me on the back and said, "There's a good fellow," and Ted said, "Go down there, and don't pull your punches."

This was most unwelcome. Alerting others to the error of their ways was something Wolff enjoyed. Not me. People don't always welcome this kind of intervention, it is my experience. They tend to turn nasty.

"He may get violent," I said. "Don't you think you should come along as well?"

But no one thought that such a good idea.

"Things like this are best settled man to man," said Ted. "If we all went, we'd just complicate things."

"Oh, and something else," said Sarah. "He's been calling us tourists. Tell him we're not."

"What are we then?" said her husband. "The Scott expedition?"

We weren't that, either, so "tourists" was allowed to stand.

On the way downstairs, I made a discovery. I was hopping mad. That bloody man was acting like a thug. He had hounded us, and ridiculed us, and lied to us. And now, here he was again—hounding us once more. Who did he think he was?

"Where are the others?" he demanded when he saw me.

"They won't be coming," I said.

On the stairs, I had wanted to hit him. But seeing him now—his nose twitching, and still in that ridiculous coat—I felt a twinge of pity. Perhaps he didn't know he was being such a pest. Maybe if I explained . . .

So I said something about tourists being a sorry lot, and there being many reasons not to like them. They were shrill and exacting, suspicious and silly, rude and overbearing. Tourists were easy to hate. But that didn't mean they *should* be hated. Life presented us all the time with people we didn't like. This was life's great challenge. It wasn't enough to love just those who deserved our love. (And God knows, we failed them all too often.) It was also our duty to love those who didn't.

I had found my stride now and might have continued for some time if the man in the coat hadn't started to glower. When Wolff took to task the brigands who crossed his path, as often as not they squeezed his hand and begged to be forgiven. Not this man. Instead of squeezing *my* hand, he was squeezing his—the way one does before one throws a punch.

"I don't like you," he said. "I've never liked you. You're a troublemaker. I knew it the moment I saw you."

It was I who had instigated this rebellion, he said, still flexing his knuckles. It was I who had turned the others against him. Well, we could turn against him, if we wanted to. It was all the same to him. He was washing his hands of us. We could fend for ourselves.

The others, when I reported this conversation, said we were well rid of him and, after much talk of narrow escapes and close shaves, we walked into town in search of something to eat.

If there isn't much to see in Kahta, it's because there isn't much of Kahta to see. On the map, KAHTA is printed in large letters, making one expect a place of considerable size. And in a way its size *is* considerable—inasmuch as everything else in the area is not. This is a quirk of Turkish cartography. Because much of Anatolia is sparsely populated, the importance of what settlements there are tends to be exaggerated.

Consisting of several modest hotels alternating with several modest restaurants, Kahta lacked distinction. Strung along a major highway, it didn't even impress as Turkish. There were no twisting lanes, no jutting minarets, no creaking carts. One didn't linger in Kahta. There was no reason to. It was a tourist town—a place where the traveler refreshed himself—and then moved on.

Over dinner, we were approached by a driver who asked if we were going to Nemrut, and when we said we were, he said he'd be happy to take us there. His price seemed a little high, but we engaged him, anyway. It was worth it, we said. We were dealing the man in the coat a setback.

The driver promised to pick us up at midnight. Because Nemrut affords a commanding view—it is some 10,000 feet above the sea—it has become the custom to make one's way to the top in the dead of night and wait for the sun to rise.

Nemrut is the site of the tomb of King Antiochus of Commagene. With its huge stone heads ringing the base of the king's burial mound, it brings to mind Shelley's "Ozymandias":

> Nothing beside remains. Round the decay
> Of that colossal Wreck, boundless and bare
> The lone and level sands stretch far away.

Sad to say, I saw none of this because when the bus arrived shortly after twelve, I was prevented from boarding. I wasn't welcome, said the driver, looking uncomfortable. And when I asked him why, he said he was following orders.

"Whose orders?"

"Erek's," he said. "The man in the coat."

"What has he got to do with it?"

"I work for him."

So much for our blow for freedom!

The others were furious. If I couldn't go, they said, they wouldn't go, either.

"Then don't go," said the driver. "But don't expect your money back."

"We'll go to the police," said Benny.

But the driver wasn't moved, telling us, in effect, to go to the police if that was what we wanted; he didn't see it doing us much good.

The student could ill afford this loss, so I insisted that they make the trip without me. I didn't really care to see Nemrut, I told them. Which was not entirely true. But I wasn't too put out. To be honest, I dreaded having to stand on that mountaintop in the freezing cold. I would be spared that, at least. So they left, promising to raise a great hue and cry when they got back, while I, for my part, returned to a nice, warm bed.

When I came down for breakfast, Erek was waiting in the restaurant. He was looking embarrassed.

"I've been thinking about what you said," he mumbled. "About the tourists? Let me buy you a glass of tea."

It was an attempt at reconciliation, and we had breakfast together. I ended up quite liking him. Behind all that posturing, he was fairly decent.

Tourism in Kahta—as in many towns in this part of Turkey—was controlled by a mafia, he said. In Kahta, the syndicate was headed by a godfather who so feared for his safety he had recently hired a second bodyguard. Kahta, said Erek, was a town divided. There were those who supported the godfather, and those who wanted him dead.

"We're all at each other's throats," he said. "It's better in the winter. We get along when the tourists aren't here."

He offered to drive me to Nemrut that afternoon. To compensate.

"It'll cost you nothing," he said. "I'll borrow a car."

"That's very nice of you, but I don't have the time. When the others get back, we're going to Cappadocia. To Urgup."

"But that's great," he said. "I've got a girlfriend there. I'll go with you. Have you hired a driver? No? Then leave that to me. I'll take care of everything."

He stood up to go.

"You know," he said, "I've had two bad days so far this season. Yesterday was one of them."

Little did either of us know that the third would come so quickly.

———

The trip to Urgup began pleasantly enough. We were late leaving. First, the minivan developed a minor problem. And then Erek— the new Erek—announced that he couldn't go anywhere without washing his hair. There was a further delay while he searched for his shampoo. When he couldn't find it, I let him borrow mine.

But no one seemed to mind these setbacks. Erek, in high spirits now, was showing himself to have a lot of charm. On the way out of town, his hair still wet, he regaled us with a selection of Turkish folk songs. I thought he sang them rather well.

He winked in my direction. "In Urgup," he said, "you and I are going to a discotheque. To pick up women."

The former enemies were now collaborators.

We stopped by the roadside to eat a picnic lunch. There were biscuits and chick-peas and rather a lot of melons. When we'd bought them four days earlier, those melons had seemed like a good idea. Now, they'd become a burden. No one wanted the trouble of carrying them.

"Why don't you give them away?" said Erek.

Which was what we did—to a group of five Kurdish women keeping an eye on a flock of goats. And not a moment too soon, because a day or two more and those melons would have started to decompose, and we would have found ourselves, a little like Pietro della Valle, crossing Anatolia with several rotting carcasses.

While chatting with these women, I let it slip that Sarah was a doctor. A mistake because she was promptly besieged. One woman had a lump on her head, another complained of an earache, the third had something the matter with her leg, the fourth couldn't move her finger—she may have broken it—and the fifth had cataracts.

Turks often turn to Europeans for medical assistance. In Doubayazit, I had a man show me a swelling in his groin that I hoped was just a rupture; and in Van, another man, this one very old, asked for something to ease his rheumatism. I explained as gently as I could that swellings and aching joints were not my province, though neither seemed inclined to believe me. Medicine is thought by many in rural Turkey to be part of the European syllabus—a misconception that Burnaby and his ilk did much to foster.

Before leaving for Khiva, Burnaby bought lots of Cockle's pills, "a most invaluable medicine and one which I have used on the natives of Central Africa with the greatest possible success." He once prescribed Cockle's pills for an Arab sheik. "The marvellous effects produced upon [his] mind and body . . . will never fade from my memory; and a friend of mine who passed through the same district afterwards, informed me that my fame as a 'medicine man' had not died out, but that the marvellous cure was even then a theme of conversation in the bazaar."

Warburton was another who liked to practice medicine. On the Nile, when his crew was found to have ophthalmia, he made a solution using sulphate of zinc. "Every morning and evening for a week, I had half a score of anxious eyes gazing through their films at my 'prentice hand, as it applied the magic drop. Strange to say, it cured them."

After that, the 'prentice hand grew daily bolder, and his reputation increased. Whenever he went ashore, "the halt, and maimed, and blind, swarmed around me, and were only too happy to get a bit of sticking-plaster for a consumption, or a rhubarb pill for a broken limb."

He didn't consider that this was irresponsible. Quite the contrary. According to him, he "gave hope," as he put it, to half of Egypt.

There was no limit to what the foreigner was thought able to accomplish. When Burnaby was in Erzurum, a young officer committed suicide. "The body is quite cold," Burnaby was told. "If the Effendi were to go there, perhaps he might bring it to life again."

In Bokhara, Wolff, too, was asked if he could raise the dead to life. His reply was a model of circumspection. With God's help, he said, a man might do anything he pleased.

Offering what advice she could, Sarah extricated herself, and we were on our way once more. But this trip was to be a series of delays. About thirty minutes later, our progress was halted yet again. On the road ahead of us, a crowd of some twenty people had surrounded a large, black car and were pounding its roof with their fists.

"They're going to turn that car over," said Benny. "I think they're bandits."

The student scrambled to hide his camera.

"Just pray," I said, "they don't stick thorns in your genitals."

Erek laughed.

"Relax," he said. "It's just a wedding."

The bride hailed from a nearby village, we learned later, and her neighbors had stopped the entourage to pay their respects. The newly married couple sat in the backseat, grinning broadly. The bride was dressed in white and looked quite beautiful. In the space normally reserved for a license plate, their car bore the words, in Turkish, HAPPY FOREVER.

Erek drew his fur-lined coat around him and snorted when he saw this. He was not, we were given to understand, the marrying kind.

Back on the road, it became apparent that the driver was less than happy. He hadn't driven this route before, he said. Which I could well believe. From the tentative way he was acting, I would say that the routes he had driven were few. The man was obviously a novice.

"Erek," said Ted, "I know your friend needs the practice, but could we please have a driver who knows what he's doing?"

When it began to get dark, he became even more alarmed, and soon the man was driving at a crawl. He seemed especially afraid of nighttime traffic, slowing—if one *can* slow when one is inching along like this—when anything approached from the other direction.

"Can't we go any faster?" asked Benny. He was tall and thin and blond. In this gloom, he looked as amorphous as a poltergeist. "We'll never get there at this rate."

For my part, I was prepared to give him all the time in the world. Made to choose between arriving on schedule and arriving intact, I'll pick the latter. But I was alone in this opinion, the others being of the view that we had been driving long enough, and it was high time we got to bed.

"When will we get to Urgup?" Erek was asked.

"One hour," he said.

Two hours later, with Urgup nowhere in sight, we inquired again. The answer came back as before.

"One hour."

After that, it seemed better not to ask.

Once, the driver swerved suddenly, and we would almost certainly have come to grief if Erek, with great presence of mind, hadn't grabbed the wheel and guided us back to safety. To avoid similar incidents, the driver now confined himself to the middle of the road. Sarah was dismayed. "He's going to kill us," she said.

"Don't worry," I said. "There are three lanes."

"I know," she said, "but two of them are coming this way."

She was right, by God. He *was* going to kill us.

"You're in the wrong lane," Ted shouted, as a car came hurtling towards us. Erek grabbed the wheel again, and the car spend past, its horn blaring.

"What's the matter with you?" Ted demanded. "Are you mad?"

It was one of a number of questions put to the driver over the next few hours.

He was questioned about his competence: "Have you any idea what you're doing?" Questioned about his sanity: "Are you sure you're all there?" Questioned about his intelligence: "What are you? Some kind of nitwit?"

Questions were raised about his faculties: "Are you blind or what?" About his intentions: "Are you trying to give us a heart attack?" About his familiarity with his own minivan: "Don't you know you have a turn signal?"

He also received a number of instructions. "Get a move on." (A special favorite, this.) "Slow down." (A close runner-up.) And then, in descending order of popularity, "Watch where you're going"; "Brake when you take that curve"; "Pass that car"; "Use your horn"; "Look in your mirror."

Poor man! Think of it: not *one* backseat driver, but five. By now, he was shaking so badly that even Erek was moved to pity.

"Pull over here," he said. "I'll drive for a while."

But Erek, it turned out, drove even more erratically—on top of which he was speeding to make up for lost time.

The chorus of complaint began anew, augmented by the driver so recently usurped. Now that he was relieved of his command, this man's confidence magically returned, and soon he was denouncing Erek as fiercely as the rest of us. Erek was a hothead, he said. He was reckless. And what was more, he had no regard for the safety of his passengers. It was all to no avail. Erek pretended to hear none of it.

We had entered an area of low hills, and the road, climbing now and much narrower, had become serpentine. Curve followed curve in quick succession. It was pitch black. The headlights began to flicker, but Erek didn't slacken speed. Another curve. And another. And then the headlights failed completely, and we were hurtling along unable to see a thing.

The van struck something—a boulder, we discovered later—and Erek hit the brakes. The vehicle swerved violently, and then we were plunging off the road and into a ditch. We might have overturned if—mercy of mercies—we hadn't struck a tree.

There was a moment's silence, and then there was bedlam. People shouted and cursed and issued threats as they scrambled from the van—no easy matter since it was wedged against that tree. Miraculously, no one was hurt.

Erek sidled up to me in the darkness. "Remember that glass of tea we had after our fight?" he said. "We may have to have another."

"Look down there," said the student. On the other side of the road lay a black abyss. "That's a drop of a hundred feet."

We'd had a narrow escape, but instead of being thankful, Ted became enraged.

"That does it," he said. And leaping at Erek, he grabbed him by the throat. It took two of us to pry them apart.

"I'm glad you did that," Erek said later. "I'm a boxer, you know. I wouldn't want to hurt him."

It had turned quite cold.

"Where are we?" said Sarah.

"Miles from anywhere," said Benny.

"Well, we can't spend the night here," she said. "We'll freeze to death."

With much straining and pushing, we managed to get the van back onto the road.

"Shall I drive?" asked Erek.

"You'll do nothing of the sort," said Ted. "I'm taking charge."

In disgrace now, Erek and his colleague were relegated to the backseat, where they sat like chastened children. In effect, we had commandeered their van.

The van started readily enough, and the headlights chose to work, but we had advanced no more than a mile when Ted announced he could go no farther. The brakes were acting up, he said, and the steering, as he put it, was "buggered." Since our way now lay downhill, it was deemed too dangerous to proceed. We got out again—this time to walk.

It wasn't pleasant stumbling along in the dark like that, lugging our bags and chilled to the bone. To improve the mood, I suggested playing Capital Cities, but it had to be abandoned when we got to *P*. Sarah had suggested *Peking,* but her husband said this was unacceptable because *Peking* was now *Beijing,* at which point Sarah accused him of being unreasonable and withdrew from the game.

So then I had us recite our favorite poems, and Ted kicked off with "Lepanto."

White founts falling in the Courts of the sun,
And the Soldan of Byzantium is smiling as they run;
There is laughter like the fountains in that face of all men
    feared,
It stirs the forest darkness, the darkness of his beard.

He had reached the bit about Don John of Austria riding to the sea when we chanced on a roadhouse. Inside, a group of men were engaged in an all-night revel. The floor was littered with empty beer bottles, and the air was thick with male camaraderie.

Not a woman in sight. They stood up and stretched when we entered, seeming neither to mind this intrusion nor to see anything unusual in it. To look at them, you'd think that cold, bedraggled strangers stumbled in here all the time.

The proprietor, after telephoning to Urgup, said a van was on its way to pick us up.

"A *real* van," he said with a look at Erek. "With a *real* driver."

Tea was summoned, and a plate of soft, musty-smelling biscuits was passed around. Erek went outside to urinate, and the driver used the opportunity to tell me what a scoundrel he was.

"He's completely dishonest," he said. "Believe nothing he says. He's a bad man. I'm sorry you had to meet him."

Then the driver left to urinate, and it was Erek's turn to level accusations. The driver had misled him, he said. He had presented himself as a man with extensive experience. How was he to know that he was lying?

"I'm too trusting," he said. "People use me."

He glanced at his watch. "It's too late to go a discotheque now," he said, sighing. "I washed my hair for nothing."

The ride to Urgup in the new van took two hours. It was almost dawn when we fetched up at the Hotel Kismet. Erek stood by the door, his eyes cast down, and shook each of us by the hand as we entered. The owner, a charming old man who had heard about our "bad experience," said he was dispensing with passport formalities. We would be shown upstairs right away. We were all of us exhausted.

It was 5:10 when I got to my room, and 5:12 when I got to bed. At 5:13, I was fast asleep.

After that, Cappadocia proved something of an anticlimax. It was spectacular, of course. How could it *not* be? A layer of tufa covers this part of Turkey. (Our guide, whose English wasn't very good, referred to it as "tofu.") Tufa is soft, which means that wind and rain can do with it what they please. And what wonders they have wrought! In Cappadocia, one has the sensation of visiting a vast sculpture garden whose curator has a special fondness for the work of Henry Moore.

There are towers here, and steeples, and pillars, and cones. One pillar had what looked like a horse on top; another had a bear. On a third was an eagle with its wings spread wide. There were cockerels, too, and dinosaurs, and jaguars, and huge, huge mushrooms.

The cones predominated. The area around Urgup fairly bristled with them. Cones red and purple and pink and gold, they climbed, some of them, to heights of over ninety feet. These were the fairy chimneys for which Cappadocia is famous, and they reminded one of nothing so much as the spires of Gaudi's cathedral in Barcelona.

It was extraordinary—and yet I found it impossible to be moved by any of it. Why is that? On some days, one is touched by everything; on others, paradise itself would fail to stir one's interest.

The two things I remember about that day had nothing to do with Cappadocia's landscape. The first occurred when I left my bag in a teahouse. An hour elapsed before I missed it. And though it contained my passport, my money, my credit cards, my camera, and all my notebooks, this being Turkey, I never doubted it was safe. We drove back and there it was, exactly where I remembered putting it.

"Is it yours?" said the waiter. "I was watching it for you."

The other memory was provided by our guide. A short, stout man with glasses much too big for him, he took us through hills folded like pink meringue to Scarlet Valley, there to see the sun set. No one loves sunsets more than a tour operator. They're another way to pad an itinerary. And, best of all, they don't cost a penny.

I bought us several bottles of wine, one of which I gave to the guide. I imagined he would take it home. Instead, he opened it then and there and consumed it on the spot. It made him tipsy, and he began to declaim on the Turk's love of nature.

"The nature in Cappadocia is wonderful," he said. "The sun, the flowers, the trees—these things are very special to us. They are in our hearts. Do you understand?"

"Yes," I said. "They are special to us, too."

He looked at me askance.

"I'm sorry," he said. "I find that hard to believe. May I have some of your wine?"

After that, we threw stones at a wishing hole in a fairy chimney. When I threw mine, I dislodged a stone already inside.

"Now look what you've done," said the guide. "You've eaten someone else's wish. Is there any more of that wine?"

Back in Urgup, he struggled out of the van and fell flat on his face. It was the very first time I'd seen a Turk get drunk.

———

I didn't ever see Erek after he shook our hands that night of our arrival. But I did hear of him—twice. Two days later, we ran into his driver. He was looking dejected. He and Erek were to have returned to Kahta that morning, he said, but the trip had been canceled when Erek failed to show up. He was seeing a woman, said the colleague—someone he'd met in a discotheque—and was off somewhere drinking deeply from pleasure's cup.

"I'll just have to wait," said the driver. "I can't go anywhere without him. He has my money."

A day after this encounter, Benny ran across our nemesis near the citadel. Erek was drunk. And very hostile. Love had done nothing to improve his disposition.

"Someone put you up to this, didn't they?" he demanded.

"Up to what?" said Benny.

Erek snorted.

"As if you didn't know. You're not tourists. None of you. You're mafia. You were sent here to ruin me."

And wrapping his coat tightly around him, he stormed off with the purpose of a man who knew where he was going and didn't at all fear getting there.

"A quixotic fellow," said Benny. "What does this say about the Turkish character?"

Probably, nothing at all. Awful things have been said about the Turks. In the last century, travelers routinely referred to them as terrible, lazy, unspeakable, libidinous, unconscionable, and full of treachery. Nor were they said to be very smart. When it comes to intelligence, David Hogarth wrote in 1896, the Turk "takes a rank a grade below his dog."

All nonsense, of course. Too much is made of national character. The Irish drink too much; Scots are frugal; and Swedes are dour. But are they? Are the Irish drunkards? Certainly none I know—and I know many. More accurate is this: *some* of the Irish drink too much. But even that would have to qualified. *Some* of the Irish drink too much *sometimes*. But to say that is to say nothing. Some English drink too much sometimes, too. And some French. And some Germans. . . . National types are a fiction for the reason that each of us is unique. We typify no one but ourselves—and sometimes, we don't even do that.

Mansfield Parkyns warned against the dangers of generalizing. "The opinion one may form of a people from a few glaring instances of crime, or even of valor or benevolence," he wrote, "ought not to be criterions for the entire nation."

Unlike Erek, who regretted ever laying eyes on us, the sentimental owner of the Hotel Kismet wept to see us leave. When we told him that his hotel was *cok guzel* (beautiful) and Urgup was *cok guzel,* he said we were *cok guzel,* too. It brought a lump to my throat.

Tears coursing down his face, he stood at the door and waved as we left for the bus station.

"Enjoy Antalya," he called to me.

"Enjoy Konya," he called to the others.

He was still waving when we turned a corner and were lost to view. Such a nice old man. I wish now I'd let him squeeze my nipple when he tried to. Where was the harm in it?

chapter 9

I met my second Turkish drunk in Antalya. This one was a bootblack whose place of business was a huddle of palm trees overlooking the harbor. He looked like a mole—sloping shoulders and a long nose and eyes that appeared curiously naked because he had no lashes. He filled a tea glass from a bottle of raki he kept in his pocket. He drained the glass, filled it again, and handed me the bottle. It was not yet noon. A little early for raki. I told him I didn't drink.

My shoeshine took an age because, quite intoxicated, he did everything twice. He cleaned my shoes; polished them; brushed them; buffed them; and then, just when I thought him finished, the sequence was repeated.

But what really slowed things down was his ogling. Each time a woman passed, he'd extend his tongue and whimper with lust. He seemed not to care how these women looked. Young or old, plain or fancy, his response was always the same. Unless they were fat. He had a fondness for fat. At the sight of one plump matron, he stuck a hand down his trousers and pretended to masturbate.

Then the police turned up, and the women were forgotten. To disguise the smell of raki, he reached for a bowl of yoghurt—strategically placed for just such an emergency—which he now consumed in heaping spoonfuls. He even had me eat some—to make the charade more plausible, I suppose. All unnecessary, it turned out. The police, who had warned him not to drink in public, had come to chase away some peddlers, and they paid us not the slightest heed.

When they left, he asked if I had "woman books," and then he brought up Holland. Holland, with its liberal sexual attitudes, occupies a special place in the Turkish imagination. Was it true, the bootblack wanted to know, that sex in Amsterdam was now compulsory?

"Absolutely," I said. "Unless you can get a medical exemption. Poor eyesight. Flat feet. Asthma. That sort of thing."

But he didn't see the joke.

"What a place," he said. "Men dress as women, women dress as men, and homosexuals everywhere."

Not that he had anything against homosexuals, he was careful to add. We had the right, all of us, to sleep with whom we pleased. Didn't I agree?

His tone grew confidential, and he poured himself more raki. He was not a Moslem, he said; he smoked and drank, and had sex whenever it chanced along. And not just with women. With men, too, sometimes. He paused. A significant pause. I knew what was coming.

"Do *you* like men?" he resumed.

"Good Lord," I said, pretending to notice the time. "I'm late for an appointment. I have to get going."

He wouldn't let me leave until I'd kissed him à la Turque.

"Come back tomorrow," he called after me. "We can go for a swim."

Normally, these approaches are no more consequential than that. But a day later, something out of the ordinary happened.

Down in the harbor, I met a man who wanted to know if I'd seen the caves. He had brown hair and blue eyes and didn't look Turkish at all. A small wart grew on his upper lip.

"Caves?" I said.

They were farther along the coast, he explained, and had once been used as oratories. In some, the walls had been painted.

"How odd," I said. "My guidebook makes no mention of them."

"That's because few people know they're there. Would you like me to drive you? It isn't far."

Our route took us inland and included two stops: one at a newsstand for cigarettes and one in a service station for gas. My companion seemed in no great hurry, and I wondered briefly if there really were caves. And then we came in sight of the sea and turned along the coast.

He stopped the car. "We're here," he said, grinning.

He scrambled down a cliff, and I scrambled after him. He was faster than I was. But then, it struck me later, in all probability he had done this before. He ducked into a cave, and I followed, and there he was, still grinning and with his trousers about his knees. He was wanking furiously.

When I drew back in surprise, he indicated that I should join him in this activity, and when I declined, he got angry—livid, actually—and made personal remarks, none of which were true. Well, almost none. He was clearly not a person who liked to be thwarted.

He was up the cliff before I was, and he beat me to the car. By the time I made it over the brow, he had driven off. I had to hitch back to Antalya—a distance of thirty miles. But I did have one consolation. When we'd stopped in that service station, I'd been tempted to pay for the gasoline. Imagine how I'd feel if I had!

It was a curious experience, and he was a curious fellow.

Whatever possessed him? And why pick me? Did I look like someone who masturbates in caves? Who bares his genitals on demand? I didn't really think so. Why, then? What had made him do this? Did he need sex so badly he would take his chances with a stranger? Was he really that desperate?

It was certainly possible. Turkish men are a desperate lot, and it's all the fault of religious stricture. The segregation of the sexes is so Draconian in much of this country that men and women, until they marry, seldom come in contact. In much of rural Turkey, it's a rare thing to see a woman in public.

"Do you like our women?" Ahmet had asked me in Van. I was hard put to say. Though I'd been in Van a week, I had seen very few.

"Where do they take themselves?" I asked. "How do they spend their time?"

"They stay at home," he said.

"By choice?"

"I think so. They feel safe at home. They're out of harm's way."

When women must venture out, many do so in chador—wrapped in black from head to foot. "Coffin-like bundles," King-lake called them, and there is a touch of the sinister about them. Not even the eyes are visible. There's something chilling about this debasement. These crowlike figures don't seem human at all. One man told me that women lack souls. When he got to paradise, he said, he no more expected to see his wife than he did his favorite dog.

One sees women in the company of women, but rarely in the company of men—unless they happen to be relatives. And then, the woman's presence is peripheral. Doomed to do little more than hover, she reminds one of a satellite trapped forever in the orbital pull of a more powerful neighbor. Trailing after her menfolk, she doesn't speak, and she isn't consulted. These men seem unaware of her. So little heed is she paid, they might have forgotten she exists at all.

On the way to Antalya, our bus stopped for a family waiting by the roadside. First the men got on; then several young boys; and finally, the woman in the group, dressed in black and virtually ignored. I do believe that had the bus gathered speed suddenly and left her behind, not one of them would have noticed.

On the bus, the men and children seated themselves quickly enough. The woman, though, just gazed about her. She was at a loss. It was not that there weren't any seats. There were several. And that was the problem. She couldn't choose between them.

She gazed until her husband noticed her dilemma. "There," he said, pointing to a sack in the aisle. And "there" was where she placed herself, glancing to neither left nor right for the rest of the journey.

It was all quite shocking, and one was left to wonder if people who are prevented from thinking don't, in time, lose the ability. And what happens once they do? Can this capacity ever be revived? Can one's existence afterwards ever be more than animal?

It's unusual to see a woman in a teahouse. Turkey's great gathering points are male preserves, places where men may revel in the company of other men. And how they revel! They kiss when they meet and shake hands, the handshake not released immediately, but held, the link maintained, the contact obviously relished.

All that camaraderie! Everyone talking at once, everyone laughing. In the beginning, I envied them. Why can't I get along like this with *my* male friends? I asked myself. Until I remembered the price they pay for this intimacy—the loss as measured in the relationships they might be having. After that, I didn't envy them so much.

In Istanbul, the men I got to know never brought their wives when we met in the evenings. Instead, they'd turn up making their excuses. "My wife can't come. One of the children has a cold." Or "My wife can't come. Her mother hurt her ankle."

So many colds. So many twisted ankles. Is the Turkish climate so treacherous? The Turkish home so fraught with peril? The truth, I suspect, is that their wives were never asked. Men have come to prefer the company of other men. Their contacts with other males are familiar and comfortable and easy to predict. Not so their contacts with women. Women puzzle them. (Since the sexes seldom mix, how could they not?) They regard them as an unknown species—foreign, hard to gauge, difficult to trust.

There's nothing necessarily sexual about this bonding. While homosexuality is often described as "prevalent" in the East, just what is meant by *prevalent* is never specified. (Is there a place where homosexuality is not prevalent?) Instead, the literature abounds with vague references to "the vices and depraved habits to which Orientals are so addicted."

In Khiva, Burnaby tells us, "good-looking boys of an effeminate appearance, with long hair streaming down their shoulders, and dressed a little like the women, lounged about, and seemed to have nothing in particular to do." Perhaps they *did* have nothing in particular to do—again this irritating, and disingenuous, Victorian coyness. Clearly, though, this is not what Burnaby would have us believe. We are to understand that these effeminate boys didn't always lounge, that once in a while, they saw employment.

In the virtual absence of women, men will turn to one another more than they would were women more available. Men have sex with men not out of preference, as some writers claim, but because they have little choice. While Turkish women may be "too degraded for respect"—I am quoting Palgrave—they are far from being "too despised for love."

A woman I met in Istanbul told of being on a bus when the

teenager next to her reached across and fondled her knee. Gently, she removed his hand. But moments later, it was back.

"I'm a grandmother," she told him. "I'm sixty years old."

The boy smiled graciously. "That's OK," he said. "I don't mind."

Another woman—this one in Antalya—explained why she so looked forward to the summer. In June, the city filled with females from the boreal north. Lusty Germans looking for sun and sex. Antalya's women could enjoy a respite. "For three months," she said, "we're left alone. The winters here are miserable."

Summer was winding down when I got to Antalya. I didn't mind. I was glad to have left the Anatolian plateau. After a month in that semidesert, I'd begun to feel depressed. But heading south from Urgup, I felt my spirits lift. The land was green again. We drove through fertile plains where bananas grew, and verdant valleys where women gathered grapes. We'd entered a gentler realm.

Behind Antalya's harbor—a small cove of turquoise water—stood the old city walls, castellated in parts and punctuated by an occasional tower. The walls aside—a constant in this country's urban architecture—little here was distinctly Turkish. The character was more Mediterranean. There are towns like this in Greece and Spain and Italy.

Across the bay were slabs of rock the color of smoked salmon. Behind them was a line of mountains. *Pink* mountains, but no less fierce for that. Up, up, they soared, as if straining to outdo one another. In nature, competition is rife. Definitely Gothic, those peaks: serrated tops, and crags, and summits edged with cloud. Sometimes I gazed at them for hours.

The harbor was lined with palm trees, their trunks curving gently, their fronds exploding like paper flowers pulled from a conjurer's hat. The bay sparkled so much, it might have been covered with rhinestones.

Several big yachts lay at anchor. Their crews worked tirelessly: swabbing decks, painting hatches, checking rigging, oiling engines. All that activity suggested they might be going somewhere. Yet nothing ever came of these exertions. In the week I spent in Antalya, not one of these boats ever put to sea.

The day of my arrival, I went to the harbor to watch the sun go down. I was early—sunset was a good two hours away. But what did it matter? I had all the time in the world. Besides, there was tea to drink. Nothing fills an hour like tea. And after that? Who knew? I'd stopped planning ahead. It was enough that the next ninety minutes would be accounted for. Why be obsessive?

Sunsets are more enjoyable than sunrises. (And not because the sun rises in what, for all practical purposes, is the dead of night.) The sun rising is brash—all thrust and vigor and overweening pride. Setting, it is something else entirely. It is spent now. It has run its course. And watching it disappear, we are reminded that, very soon, we too will fade from view. It does one good to ponder one's ultimate fate. It concentrates the mind wonderfully.

A young couple sat near me. The woman wore a drab gabardine coat, flat-heeled shoes, and stockings thick enough to conceal all hint of the flesh within. Couture does not come more nondescript, but this is how many Moslem women attire themselves. Their religion prefers it. She wore her head scarf in the prescribed Moslem manner—pulled low over her forehead lest a lock of hair should show. One of these days, a woman will dress in haste, and a rogue curl will break free from that restraining scarf, and I can only hope I'm not around when it happens because the sky will surely darken and the graves will give up their dead. (This same Moslem head scarf, denounced by Ataturk as a medieval relic, is again a common sight in Turkish cities, suggesting that some of his reforms are being eroded.)

The woman was doing a crossword puzzle, entering a word

and erasing it, entering another, and erasing that. This is how most of us do crosswords, but her husband watched her with mounting irritation. And then he could take no more. "Here," he said, snatching away the puzzle. "Let me do it."

Another woman would have snatched it back and told him to bugger off. Not this one. She didn't object at all, convinced, apparently, that he was better equipped to do a crossword than she was. Why would she think so? Who—or what—had persuaded her? Did she *need* persuading? Turkey has never placed much value on the female intellect. Perhaps she just *assumed* him to be smarter.

If this was the case, then the culture of which she was part had failed her. To the extent that it has reason to exist at all, it is the job of society to *encourage* self-esteem in its members, not to destroy it.

When the sun had set, I walked into the old town. I wanted to find a hotel. This part of Antalya is particularly lovely. White-washed houses with latticed windows and stout doors lined narrow, cobbled streets. Behind some of those doors, families ate oranges in courtyards filled with hibiscus blossoms.

On display near the tourist office were pictures of the city's hostelries—photographs of freshly made beds, of rooms filled with exotic flowers, of shower cubicles scrubbed until they sparkled. Everything attested to cleanliness and comfort and modernity. There were photographs, too, of the staff in these establishments— beaming men standing in gleaming hallways, beaming women bustling about gleaming kitchens, and beaming gardeners proudly surveying their teeming flower beds. Finally, there were photos of those for whom these kitchens and gardens were so scrupulously maintained—the guests themselves: guests self-consciously drinking tea, self-consciously watching television, self-consciously making merry with the help.

The picture this provided of Antalya's hotels was an attractive one. Accommodations were "inexpensive," boasted a "friendly atmosphere," and lay "just minutes from shops and beaches." The purveyors of this hospitality, one was to think, were the perfect hosts. They were skilled nutritionists whose menus nourished as much as they appealed to the palate; they were proficient in any language you might care to name; and they devoted their every waking moment to the comfort and repose of their guests, every one of whom, it was suggested, entered these hotels a client and left a friend.

Antalya's hoteliers may have been all these things, but they were also shrewd. One of them showed me a room costing twenty dollars.

"Is it quiet?" I said.

He took me to another room—right next door and the exact same size. "The quietest room I have," he said.

When I handed him twenty dollars, he shook his head. Quietude had a price. He now wanted thirty!

I ended up staying at the Pension Suleyman. It was beyond my means, but Meltem, the owner's daughter, made me a deal. When I said I had little money, she took me to a cheaper pension down the street. And when that proved full, she said I could sleep in the Suleyman's bar.

"Will your father mind?"

"Not if I tell him not to."

So that was where I made my bed for a week—waiting until the last revelers had left before settling down in a sleeping bag among empty bottles and unwashed glasses and enough cigarette ash to fill a bucket.

"I like to help people," Meltem said, and I didn't doubt it. She was twenty-two and beautiful. She was also short, though this I didn't notice right away because her hair, helped by lots of styling mousse, added a good three inches to her height. What I *did* notice—and notice immediately—were her eyes: light brown they were, the color of young chestnuts.

They were honest eyes. And steadfast. And I loved them. I loved everything about this person. After three months of steering clear of Turkish women—it seemed the wisest course—talking to Meltem was bliss. I found her enchanting—there's no other word for it—and I began to think that I might be in love. I was another Loti, I convinced myself. I had found my Aziyadé.

Burnaby didn't like the women in Constantinople. They "are not prepossessing," he wrote, "and sadly wanted expression—a defect which I subsequently observed in almost every Turkish woman whose countenance I had the opportunity of seeing."

But this was a dissenting view. Typically, the women of the East were found to be exquisite. This is how one fair enticer looked to Don Quixote: "She was all bedecked with pearls, which hung thick upon her head and about her neck and arms. Her feet and legs were bare, after the custom of that country, and she had upon her ankle a kind of bracelet of gold, and set with such rich diamonds that her father valued them, as she has since told me, at 10,000 pistoles a pair; and those set about her wrist were of the same value. She appeared to me the best-dressed and most beautiful woman I have ever seen; . . . she passed with me for a goddess from heaven, descended upon earth for my relief and happiness."

Far from a catalog of physical beauty, the description reads like a list of assets—something lawyers might consult when negotiating a division of property. But that's the way I imagined Meltem—bedecked with gold and pearls—as she and I hurried to our trysting place, a marble pavilion overlooking the sea. Here, as night fell, servants laid cushions for us and served us sherbet. The air was heavy with the scent of honeysuckle. Beyond the open window, water leaped from an alabaster fountain. A nightingale sang in a cypress tree.

Meltem, who had retired briefly, now returned. She was wearing not her customary skirt and blouse, but a caftan of blue silk embroidered with gold and edged with rubies. In her hair was an ostrich feather held in place by a diamond clasp. Her feet were bare. She smelled of rosewater.

Meltem put a finger to her lips. Did she hear something move in the garden? "If we're caught..." We knew what discovery meant: beheading for me; for her, a watery grave. But the garden, when I went to look, was empty. Meltem pretended to be relieved. Pretended because, in truth, we enjoyed these perturbations. The fear of being found together enhanced our pleasure. And then the servants were sent away, and there were just the two of us alone in the purple night.

Rapturous hour followed rapturous hour until—where had the time gone?—the muezzin was announcing dawn, and we were hurrying through the streets once more, hurrying to get her home before her father found her missing.

If I thought I had fallen in love, I wasn't allowed to do so for long. Meltem hated silliness. This was no Eastern voluptuary trained in the wiles of love. She was, instead, distinctly modern, and if there was to be a courtship, it would have to be modern, too.

But her father had other ideas. A man who guarded his daughter jealously, he rarely let her out of his sight. She couldn't accept my dinner invitation, she said, because he wouldn't allow it. Lunch, then? No, he wouldn't allow that, either. Perhaps tea? Out of the question.

I suggested a short walk. In broad daylight. While all of Antalya watched. She smiled sadly and shook her head. "My father thinks I'm still a child," she said.

She hated these restrictions. She more than hated them. They made her furious because she knew them to be unjust. Especially since her brother, four years her junior, was allowed to do much as he pleased. "No, not 'allowed,'" she corrected herself. "He's *encouraged*."

She sighed. "I want to marry a man with a good heart and a sense of humor," she said, "but how can I if I can't go out? It's very hard for women in Turkey. I'm trapped here. I want some opportunities. I want to go to America."

"So go."

"How? Where would I get the money? Where would I get a visa? Turks aren't liked in other countries. No one wants us."

"Then move to Istanbul. Or Ankara."

She snorted. "I've been to Ankara," she said. "It's worse than here. I wanted to buy a miniskirt. I couldn't find one."

But that was only one reason she hadn't liked it. In Ankara, she had stayed with relatives of her mother—fundamentalists. "They made me memorize the Koran. Every day for two weeks. I thought I was losing my mind."

She was grinning now and, donning a head scarf, pretended to be a *gelin*. When a girl marries in rural Turkey, she moves in with her in-laws and becomes, in effect, an unpaid servant. *Gelin* means "come," and until her husband can build her a home, it is all the young bride hears. *Gelin,* do this. *Gelin,* do that. *Gelin,* where are you?

The unfortunate *gelin* must bear this treatment with equanimity. Voice even a mild complaint, and she is deemed to have shamed her husband. In much of Anatolia, the *gelin* still leads a life of quiet desperation. Many, I was told, have nervous breakdowns.

All deference and downcast eyes, Meltem pretended to clear the table of our breakfast things. "Excuse me, effendi," she said in a tone supposed to suggest servility. Omdi, her uncle, roared with laughter.

"No, you looked at me when you took my plate," he said. "You know you're not supposed to look."

Three years older than Meltem, he, too, dreamed of escape. "Turkey is too much," he said. Turkish women, the Turkish police, Turkish politicians—he dismissed them all with a flick of his hand.

"Women are the worst. Do you know how many times I've had sex?"

"I've no idea."

"Ten times. A total of *ten* times. Can you believe that?"

I said it was hard to believe.

"There are men my age who've *never* had sex. I wouldn't either, if it weren't for the tourists. God, I look forward to the summer. The winters here are torture."

Why, then, if doing so causes such hardship, does Turkey ostracize its women? What is it about them that inspires such fear? Why would society go to such lengths to separate the sexes?

It had no choice, said Omdi. Turkish women were a wanton lot. Without surveillance, they would go to the dogs.

"I'd watch myself if I were you," he said. "No one is safe around them."

A century ago, David Urquhart had sounded just such a warning. In England, he wrote, "the men ogle the women; in Turkey, the women ogle the men. With us, the lady looks shy and bashful; in Turkey it is the gentleman."

According to Lord Kames, these putative strumpets did more than ogle. They ambushed men; they stripped them of their clothes; they had their way with them. (One of their victims was an English aristocrat whom they left with just his hat.) Eventually, Montesquieu tells us, their depredations became such a nuisance, men were moved to act. They invented the harem.

In *Don Juan,* Byron applauded this decision:

The Turks do well to shut—at least sometimes
The women up because in sad reality
Their chastity in these unhappy climes
Is not a thing of that astringent quality
Which in the north prevents precocious crimes
And makes our snow less pure than our morality.

Byron, of course, was being droll, but he was also pointing up a widely held belief: Turkish women are loose. Loti had this to say about them: they "hold fidelity to their husbands very cheap. Always idle, eaten up with ennui . . . they are capable of giving themselves to the first comer."

Capable, perhaps. But how many actually dared? Those whose indiscretions were discovered often forfeited their lives.

Omdi claimed to know a man who had drowned his unfaithful wife. "He had to," he said. "If he hadn't, her family would have drowned her."

And the police?

"They don't care. It's none of their business."

"Would you kill your wife if she slept with someone else?"

"Why not? Wouldn't I have a right?"

I could only think that the most recent of his sex partners, a woman just returned to Hamburg, had had a lucky escape.

Omdi said he felt her absence keenly. He showed me photographs of the two of them together. How happy they looked. In one, they gamboled in the surf; in another, they held hands and watched the sun set. What torture it had to be to look at these pictures. And yet how could he resist looking? That's the awful thing about photographs. As often as not, they end up mocking us.

One morning, Omdi and I were taking a walk when he

produced what he called his "comfort"—a lingerie catalog. "My constant companion," he said. "Nice, no?"

After leafing through it, he inquired about my sex life. It's hardly eventful, my sex life—though I dare say that, to him, it would sound like the Marquis de Sade's. But I didn't feel inclined to discuss it.

"Then tell me about your girlfriends," he said. "Do they like sex?"

When I declined to discuss this, too, he contented himself with leering suggestively at the women we passed. How exhausting it has to be—this obligation men feel to simulate lust whenever they see a female.

Hoping to distract him, I asked if Meltem's father wasn't being harsh. "Why won't he let her out?" I said.

"He lets her out as much as he can. If he gives her too much freedom, no one will marry her."

A boy galloped by on a snow white horse. He was decked out like a bugler: peaked hat, epaulets, a braided jacket. The uniform of those about to be circumcised. The boy was followed by another horse—this one ridden by a woman—and a cart bearing four musicians: a trombonist, two guitarists, and a man with a trumpet.

"No one *can* marry her. No one ever meets her."

"That's not a problem. Her father will find someone."

"Isn't that something she should do for herself?"

But Omdi wasn't listening. He had stopped in his tracks. "Look," he said.

A woman—an American I would guess—had stepped out of a shop and was walking just ahead of us. Her arms and legs were bare, and her cut-off T-shirt revealed much of her midriff. Her lips, visible when she glanced around, were glossed to make them look as if she'd just run her tongue over them. Her hair was artfully askew. It suggested—as no doubt it was meant to—a recent amatory tumble.

How provocative she looked. When all the women in a place dress like this, the effect loses much of its impact. Not, though, in Turkey. In Turkey, women wore camouflage when they ventured out. And Omdi, still staring, stood rooted to the spot. You'd think he'd seen a unicorn.

I began to say something, but he grabbed my arm and raised a finger to his mouth. Make a sound, he seemed to think, and this prodigy of nature would take to her heels and never be seen again. He didn't speak until the siren turned a corner and disappeared from view.

"I'm dreaming," he said. He sounded stunned. "I have to talk to her."

I tried to explain that the conventions of flight and pursuit were different in America—that there, a woman could *look* attractive without *wanting* to attract. Not, at any rate, to the extent of being followed. But he looked skeptical; he thought I was talking nonsense.

"We're wasting time," he said. "Are you coming or not?"

I gave up. "You go," I said. "I'm off to Canakkale tomorrow. I'd better book a seat on the bus."

"Canakkale?" he said.

"I want to see Troy."

I watched him hurry away. I could only hope he wouldn't find his unicorn. What would come of it if he did? Just more hand-holding and gamboling in the surf, leading inevitably to more disappointment. And nothing to show for it but another set of mocking pictures.

chapter 10

The woman in whose hotel I stayed in Canakkale was a friend of Meltem's. "She'll be glad to see you," she said. "She recently suffered a loss." A *double* loss: both her sons died in a traffic accident.

"A bus hit their motorbike," the woman told me over a glass of apple tea. One was twenty, the other twenty-two.

"Allah," she said with a brief glance at the sky. From her tone, I couldn't be sure if she blamed him for this tragedy or thought that he, alone, could fathom it.

Over dinner, the subject came up again. Her husband was sent to fetch a photo album, and pictures of the dead were passed around the table. Nice-looking men. Happy and healthy and full of life. In one picture, they posed with the motorbike on which they met their end. It had been a present to the younger when he finished school.

The death certificates were produced. And first, the old woman read them, then her daughter, and then her daughter's husband. After which, the old woman asked to read them again. There was something desperate in the way she scoured these documents. She wanted an explanation. She knew *how* her sons had died. What she couldn't understand was why.

She began to cry. A terrible thing to see, this: an old person shaking with grief. The old deserve better. At seventy, happiness should be a right. And then her daughter cried. The girl's husband patted her arm until he, too, burst into tears and had to hurry from the table. And the rest of us sat there—myself, a woman from Lyons, and a couple from Munich—sick with misery, and wishing to God there was something we might do to help. To lose one child is tragedy enough. But two! Two *grown* children. Two young adults poised to take their place in the world.

Then the old man, who usually said very little, began to speak. Offering comfort, I suppose, though he spoke quickly, and I didn't understand him. He talked and talked—Allah was invoked a lot—and one by one they dried their eyes and pocketed their handkerchiefs. And then the old lady got up and went to the kitchen. She was going to make us tea, she said. But we didn't want any. A pall of sadness had settled on the place, so we made our excuses. We were going to take a turn around the town, we explained. And with that, we fled.

"They need to be alone," said Ulrich, one of the Germans. A nice man, he spent hours every night searching the airwaves for European soccer scores. "It would have been wrong to stay."

But the truth was that all that grieving was too much for us. We stayed out for hours. Which wasn't easy. Aside from a man on a motorbike towing a resentful donkey, and a small boy who tried to entertain us by pretending to hang himself, Canakkale offered little in the way of distractions.

Its main thoroughfare runs down to the Hellespont, for years the source of its prosperity. The city once knew wealth as a customs station; today, it is supported by its fishing fleet. In appearance, it is big and nondescript. Its major commercial buildings date from the turn of the century and are in a style once favored by banks and shipping companies: stolid, dull, enduring.

"It reminds me of Liverpool," said Ulrich. "It's Liverpool without any people."

But even with people, the place seemed subdued. There was about it none of Turkey's chaotic vitality. Canakkale is prim. Respectable. There is no litter, and no starving dogs, and the people wear suits and retire at ten o'clock. Why, it doesn't even have a decent teahouse.

When we got back to the hotel, the lounge was empty.

"Listen," said Michele, the woman from Lyons. "Someone's crying."

When I went to wash, I disturbed the old woman at her ablutions. She scuttled out of the bathroom, shielding her face with a towel. But I did catch a glimpse of her eyes. They were puffed from too much weeping.

I'd met Michele in the lobby one morning and, to start with, I hadn't liked her at all. She had just arrived in Canakkale and was looking for somewhere to stay.

"So what's the report?" she demanded, in that scolding tone the French have made their signature. "Is this place any good? Is it clean? Safe? Value for money?"

"Can't say," I said. "I've just got here."

This was a lie, and I regretted it afterwards. But I hate overbearing people. I hated, too, what those questions implied— that we foreigners had to stick together. What it meant was this: we were "us," and Turks were "them." Which was not the way I had come to view them. No, she could jolly well fend for herself. Foreigners have little to fear in Turkey. They don't need advice from the likes of me.

Ulrich hadn't liked her either. "That woman seems to think that she and I have something in common," he complained. "She travels with an electric toothbrush, for God's sake. She's a tourist!"

Ulrich and I were tourists, too, of course. (By *tourist,* I mean anyone who travels with a return ticket in his pocket.) But that was not the way we saw it. This is one of the ironies of travel. Quick to categorize others, we think of ourselves as resisting categories. The tourist is always someone else.

Michele, for example, took as dim a view of Ulrich as he took of her. She said he drank too much and was far too raucous. People like him should stay at home.

"Tourists just make it hard for real travelers," she said.

"You don't see yourself as a tourist?" I asked.

"Certainly not," she said. "I'm a bohemian."

She was a short woman in her early thirties, and I ended up becoming very fond of her. She had a small face—it was shaped like an apple—and so much hair, it threatened to engulf her. She sleeked it back, and tied it back, and pinned it back. All to no avail. This hair had a mind of its own.

"But you use an electric toothbrush," I said. "That's not bohemian, is it?"

"It is if the toothbrush is stolen."

Michele was an antitourist, and this posed a bit of a problem because antitourists and tourists are hard to tell apart. They board the same buses and eat the same meals, buy the same trinkets and even sound the same complaints. How is one to distinguish them?

Easy, said Michele. The difference is one of sensibility. We had it (she was kind enough to think me an antitourist, too), and tourists didn't. That's why we were better. We were more curious. More sensitive. More alert. More frugal.

This last was especially important. The antitourist is averse to spending money. His object is to travel as far as possible as cheaply as possible. The antitourist likes to stint himself, with the result that he's apt to fall ill. But that's all to the good. There is status in sickness. It means you live rough. There is status, too, in hardship. (You haven't suffered any hardships? Then you had better invent some.) And there is status in tenure.

The time you spend in a place need not be long. What *really* matters is that you get there first. The tourists who give you pitying looks when you struggle from the bus station heavily burdened would yesterday have looked as you do now. But twenty-four hours is a long time in a tourist's life. Now they have their bearings. They've found shelter and a decent restaurant. They've been to the tourist office, and they've seen the landmarks. The more enterprising will even have stumbled on the post office. This place feels like home to them now. Of course they would look proprietorial!

I do admire the solitary traveler one sees occasionally. I travel solo, too, but never for more than a week at a time. More than a week, and I'm apt to get lonely. The objectives of travelers like me are essentially modest: a couple of months here and a couple of months there and, after that, it's home in time for Christmas dinner.

You're stuck with this timetable because you've paid an airline a large sum of money to fly you to London in early December. And though you pretend to wish you hadn't—"Really!" you tell people, "what *was* I was thinking of?"—in your heart, you're glad you did. Travel is unpredictable, and this, of course, is its great appeal. But even unpredictability can pall. After three or four months of it, I've usually had enough.

The solitary traveler—the *real* traveler—never tires of the unexpected and sets himself no time limits. His aim is to walk across Turkey or to cycle to India, and he doesn't care at all how long it takes. Six months, a year, two years: it's all the same. There's no airline ticket in *his* pocket. And what does he care if he misses Christmas? What does he care if he misses three? His agenda is dictated by the road.

This fine fellow is the spiritual heir of Burnaby and War-burton. He can draw a weather chart and construct a map. He can set a bone and treat a bedsore. He can build a fire even in a rainstorm and tell at a glance the depth of a river. There's little he can't do—record glacial action, preserve animal specimens, collect volcanic gases—and little he doesn't know. Part geographer, part botanist, part astronomer, and part a dozen other things, the lone traveler is first and foremost a polymath.

He's also resilient. He shakes off illness, rebounds from injury, and takes in stride the affronts of both man and nature. He's Byronic, a noble soul. Not for him the beaten path or the society of others. His is the road less traveled; his goal—sought like some Holy Grail—the *authentic experience.*

But the lone traveler may plod his weary way to no avail. None of us is a pioneer anymore, and the authentic experience becomes daily more elusive. The world has been too well combed. All we can do now is follow in the footsteps of those who went before.

Gone—long gone—are the days when a visitor might cause a stir. When Philip Thicknesse went to France in 1775, he chanced on a hamlet whose inhabitants had never before seen anyone from England. But even a century ago—when some of our grandparents would have been afoot—a traveler might still draw crowds. Crossing Turkey, Burnaby provoked astonishment everywhere he went. In Mudurlu, "a crowd assembled to see us depart; the people taking as much interest in an Englishman as the inhabitants of London would take in a chimpanzee or a newly arrived gorilla."

It was the same in Istanos, where "in spite of the early hour, a great many inhabitants had assembled on the house-tops to have a look at the Englishman and his party." The same, too, in Sivas, and Yuzgat, and . . . The list is endless.

No more. Today, tourists fill the Serengeti and trek the Himalayas. They visit Antarctica—planeloads of them at a time—and jostle for room on Easter Island. The people Loti called "Cookies and Cookettes"—a play on Thomas Cook—have inherited the earth.

Because a "Cookie" is rarely by himself, he's spared that great bane of travel, loneliness. In Turkey, it was always on Sundays that I felt lonely. On Sundays, Turks take themselves indoors, and one feels their absence keenly. During the week, it's possible to imagine that you've infiltrated this society—a little, anyway—become a tiny part of it. The news vendor has come to know you, reaching for your paper before you ask for it. The woman at the bank smiles in recognition when you present your traveler's check. "The usual?" asks the waiter at breakfast. Turkey, you tell yourself, has taken you to its heart.

And then Sunday rolls around, and the illusion is shattered. There is no news vendor, no bank teller, no waiter. Turkey stays home, and the streets that were once so comfortable are empty, left to you and others like you: people whose homes are somewhere else.

How intensely you feel your otherness on these occasions. How you wish to be indoors, too. But where? Indoors for you is a room in a hotel. Not a place you'd care to linger. No, there is only one indoors worthy of the name: your own home. Were you only there, you could brew a pot of your own tea, occupy your own armchair, put your feet on your own coffee table . . . I love to travel, but the pleasure it affords is never unalloyed.

———

The road to Troy was lined by apple orchards and olive trees and wrecked cars. But mostly wrecked cars. They were everywhere. Turkey's roads are a battlefield, and its motorists have claimed more victims than the massed armies of Agamemnon. But instead of making our driver more circumspect, these rotting remnants had the opposite effect. At the sight of one, he would accelerate. I can only think they offended him. The result of driver error, they put a dent in his professional pride.

I took a less charitable view when he and another bus fell into competition. Our driver enjoyed this enormously, grinning like a madman as the two buses sped along the narrow road. But that was nothing to his enjoyment when they crested a hill together and had to swerve to avoid an oncoming car. Our driver wagged a scolding finger at his rival before breaking into demented laughter.

His passengers, cringing in their seats, enjoyed it rather less. Considering that only their lives were at stake, I found it odd they would be so grudging.

I thought of the old couple at the hotel. I thought of their grief and the death certificates. All brought about by a bus. A bus like this one. And a driver like this one. Cresting a hill too fast because it made him feel more of a man. The motorbike in his path suddenly. But seeing it too late. The screech of brakes. The impact. And then two men lying dead. Two men who left home, not to die, but to buy a loaf of bread. I despise whatever impulse it is that makes people behave like this. Let them kill themselves, if they feel they have to. They mustn't be allowed to endanger others.

The plains of Troy spread before us, green and gold, while in the distance, the channel called the Hellespont gleamed like the armor of Achilles.

"*Cok guzel*," said the Turk beside me. It was as much a question as it was a statement. Like many of his countrymen, he had the idea that foreigners are hard to please.

It *was* beautiful, but I couldn't enjoy it. The driver had ruined the day for me, and, like Achilles, I brooded over my anger.

"There's no silence in you," said Ulrich when we got to Troy. "What's the matter?"

He meant I seemed agitated. But what an interesting way to put it! There *wasn't* any silence in me. And silence was what I wanted just then. Actually, silence was all I ever wanted. If you had silence, you needed little else. Its silence was the thing I liked most about Turkey. The silence in Ani. The silence of Anatolia. Most of all, the silence in Turks themselves. The kind of silence that only comes when you've learned to accept your fate. Unlike me, Turks are patient.

There was no silence in Troy. The place was full of tourists—the sort Michele believed to lack sensibility—and they trooped through the ruins looking none too happy. Several of them peered into a cistern, but it was its depth—not its age—that seized their interest.

"You could hurt yourself if you fell in there," said one of them.

"Any questions?" asked their guide, a man who held a red folder above his head to distinguish himself from other guides holding other folders. But there were no questions. And no photographs except the ones they took of one another.

"I have to say I'm disappointed," said a woman. "I expected more than bits of walls and scraps of houses."

A sound from their bus—an involuntary spasm of the air brakes—and they started to run. Scrambling for seats, they reminded me of those characters in the *Iliad*, fighting "with might and main."

I felt sorry for them. Shooed from site to site at someone else's pace, they couldn't respond to anything they saw. There wasn't the time. Nor could they recall it at their leisure. The tourist doesn't have leisure. There is too much ground to cover. So the juggernaut lurches on, and novelty replaces novelty so predictably that, in time, they lose their surprise. A marvel in a series of marvels is no longer something to wonder at. It has become a commonplace.

This sort of treatment will sour the gentlest nature. I blame haste for most of our problems. Conduct your life at a pell-mell pace, and you begin to feel put upon, victimized. And that bodes ill for all of us. Generosity of spirit is rare in the victim.

Besides, something awful happens when people go about in groups. When the individual yields to the common interest, a coarsening occurs. The human desire to be liked—to get along with others—is an excellent thing, and no doubt saves all of us a lot of trouble. But if getting along means being agreeable all the time—if it means stifling one's reservations and conforming to the general will—then I see little virtue in it. No virtue at all, actually. Only danger. Pursue the common good long enough and *everyone* comes to grief.

Not a lot remains of Troy. There are no grand temples there, no mighty citadels. Just this overgrown site still in the throes of excavation. Gone is Priam's noble palace "with its portals and galleries of polished stone." Gone, too, the mansion of Paris, "a fine place built by the best workmen in the land." All gone.

I pondered, as one is supposed to on these occasions, the sadness of the passing hour and the futility of man's ambition. But I wasn't responding today—blame that idiot driver—and hard as I tried, the melancholy wouldn't come. So goeth the glory of the world, yes, but then so goeth everything. Troy was no more, but it had once been mighty. It had once been grand. Wasn't that recompense enough? Most of us never know glory, though we face extinction, too. What will be our compensation?

I sat under an olive tree and tried to summon the grandeur that was Troy. Of all the cities "built under the stars of heaven," Homer tells us, it was the one that Zeus loved most. But that was before the Greeks came, "eager to tear the Trojans to pieces." Some

27,000 Greeks. So many that "the ground thundered terribly under the tramp of horses and of men." And Helen, in Priam's palace, gazed down on them and longed "for her husband of the old days, for home and family."

I tried to summon all of this—and failed. I've never much liked the *Iliad*. It's far too bloodthirsty. I failed for another reason, too. I was growing tired of antiquities. Just as Warburton had. "By this time," he wrote of his trip to Egypt, "we had been so be-templed and be-ruined, that we looked on a city of the Pharaohs with as much indifference as on a club-house in Pall Mall."

Instead of Priam's palace, all that came to mind was another siege less famous than this one, but in its way, just as mythic: the Alamo. What did Santa Anna say when his officers reported Davy Crockett's death? History, alas, doesn't tell us. But he had come to admire his opponent, so he may have spoken as Achilles did when Hector fell: "We have won a great triumph; we have killed Hector [Crockett] to whom the Trojans [Texans] prayed as if he were a god."

But all of this was whimsy. I wanted to be touched by Troy. I wanted to reflect upon the ravages of time. But to muse, one must be in the mood. And today, that mood eluded me. Was it just the driver? Or was something more involved? I had seen a lot these past four months. Perhaps I had seen enough. I was growing weary. Like Helen, pining on Priam's walls, I missed my family. It was time to think of heading home.

———

Taking a shower that night took hours.

First the water had to be heated, and this entailed changing gas cylinders. Or it would have if the "new" cylinder hadn't turned out to be empty. The old man said he would go and buy another.

I said he shouldn't bother. I could give myself a sponge bath.

But he was adamant and went to fetch his motorbike. If I wanted a shower, I would have a shower. It would mean, though, I would have to wait.

He returned an hour later looking like a human bomb. One cylinder was tied to the handlebars, a second was strapped to the seat behind him, and a third he balanced on his knees. Had he hit anything, he would, like Davy Crockett, have blown himself and Canakkale to smithereens.

The new cylinder in place, it was now time to fire the heater. This was done with great ceremony, the family breaking into applause when it roared to life.

"Good," said the old lady. "You can have your shower at nine o'clock."

It had just turned six.

Every ten minutes for the next three hours, her daughter was sent to the bathroom to test the temperature of the water and to check that the heater was burning. She would return all smiles.

"Everything all right?" her parents would ask, glancing up from the television. They were watching a film which was set in London. I was startled by how foreign it looked. Selim was right. London *was* exotic.

Did I like to shower? I was asked.

"Very much," I said.

They could understand that, they said. They liked to shower, too. Did I shower often?

"Very often," I said. "Sometimes twice a day."

And a debate ensued as to whether this was wise. So intense was their interest in this shower and so much anticipation did it stir, I began to fear that they'd want to watch me wash.

At ten minutes to nine, the daughter announced that the water should now be sufficiently hot and rose to make one last check. But there were no reassuring smiles this time. She returned wringing her hands.

"What's wrong?" said her father.

"The water pressure," she said. "It's dropped."

Her father jumped to his feet and ran to the bathroom. It was true. The water had slowed to a trickle.

"Not to worry," I said. "It'll come back."

"It may," said the old man. "Or it could stop altogether. Take a shower while you can. At least, the water's hot."

But I could tell the whole thing was ruined for them. Ruined for them because, they thought, it had been ruined for me. They had wanted me to enjoy this shower. And their exertions had been for naught.

In the middle of the shower, the water ran cold. Of course, I didn't tell them this. They were upset enough. I went back to the kitchen when I'd finished, and there they were, the three of them, staring out the window, not saying a word. They had turned off the television. The photo album lay open on the table.

"I feel so much better," I said. "Thank you for going to all that trouble."

"Did you like it?" said the old lady, smiling weakly.

"It was one of the best showers I've ever had."

"Good," said the old man. Though not with any conviction. He knew I was making it up.

That night, extra blankets were sent to my room. By way of compensation, I suppose. And also because it had suddenly turned cold. Oh, thou boreal north! How cheerless thou can be! It was almost November, so a drop in temperature was not unexpected. But that didn't make it any more welcome. I hate cold weather. Hate it with a passion. And as I lay there that night, unable to sleep because my teeth chattered, Turkey began to lose its allure.

There is nothing exotic about being cold. Cold means one thing: misery. The misery of Burnaby in Russia, "obliged to dismount and to clean out the nostrils [of his horses], which were entirely stuffed up with icicles." The misery of being unable to write because "the ink, which was frozen into a solid lump, had smashed the bottle." And the misery of a breakfast comprising a frozen block of milk "and some butter which was as hard as a billiard-ball."

The great fear was frostbite, an agonizing affliction. After just a brief exposure, Burnaby's hands felt "as if they had been plunged into some corrosive acid which was gradually eating the flesh from the bones." The pain was "more acute than anything I had hitherto experienced."

Burnaby, remember, was supposed to be the strongest man in the British army.

Soon, not only his hands, but his arms, too, "were lost to all sensation, dead to pain—dead to every sense of feeling—hanging quite listlessly by my side. . . . It was several weeks before I thoroughly recovered from the effects of my carelessness."

It's a terrifying description, and recalling it, I longed for "the dew-dropping south." Turkey in late October is too far north. I wanted to be in the tropics. In a place resounding to the cries of monkeys. A place fragrant with the smell of frangipani. I wanted nudity and laughter and . . .

For a moment, I found myself thinking of London . . .

I wanted sorcery and voluptuous nights and days full of passion and . . .

London again. Why did it come to mind just now? Ah, yes. That film on the television. Odd how attractive it had looked. I had fled London, but I wondered now if I'd been fair to it. London had become familiar—precisely what I wanted to escape. Instead of the commonplace, I wanted exoticism—the quotidian's polar opposite. Exoticism was everything I did not have. It was everything that London lacked.

Travel is all risk and novelty and wonder. It is freedom. It is revelation. It is possibility. It is a chance to explore the elsewhere—the anywhere but here.

But is "here" all that bad? London has its wonders, too. Exoticism was not what London lacked. It was what *I* lacked. And as for revelation, what was it Kafka told us? Hadn't he said that the world reveals itself to all who pay attention? Reveals itself, if we let it, in our own kitchens?

One has to learn to attend, to notice things, to see past the clutter. And that requires patience. Was I patient enough? Probably not. But I had to try. It was that or become another Loti—endlessly prowling the world, endlessly searching. Searching because it is the only thing one knows. Searching from force of habit.

epilogue

Ercuman and his staff were watching television when I got back to Istanbul. Because the set was on a shelf above their heads, they sat with their eyes raised and their mouths open. They looked like people seeing an apparition. They were watching a bad film made additionally wretched because the picture kept rolling. It would have been a small thing to adjust the set. Yet no one bothered.

Ercuman received me like a returning prodigal and made me recount all of my adventures. I even succeeded in making him laugh. For a couple of hours, I felt like Odysseus.

"So tell me," I said, when he'd finally heard enough. "What about Osman? Did you ever find him?"

Ercuman grew serious. "No word of Osman," he said, biting his lip. He seemed plumper than I remembered him. And a little more bald. "No one knows anything about him. It's almost as if he vanished."

He seemed on the verge of tears.

"I'm not surprised," he went on. "There's no room for Osman in the new Turkey. He belongs to a past the country would like to forget."

I telephoned Selim, but he'd heard nothing, either.

"Maybe he's dead," I said.

"Dead, or as good as dead. One way or another, Osman's gone."

"And taken an era with him," I said.

"Right. And not a moment too soon."

Selim had some news for me, he said. News of "a personal nature." Could I meet him for tea in the Pera Palas?

There was a message for me when I got there. Selim had been delayed. (Some emergency having to do with the government's stand on nipples.) He would join me in the pastry shop as soon as he could.

The Pera Palas was founded by a Frenchman a century ago and still affects a Gallic ambience. The pastry shop had lots of tulip sconces and ornate gilded mirrors and plants in urns of polished brass. The walls had been painted a bright peach. Dotted about the room were numerous armchairs, all offering varying degrees of concealment: chairs with canopies, chairs with wings, and chairs that sighed when you sat in them and closed around you like the limbs of a man-eating tree.

I was seated on something resembling a daybed. Several frilled cushions were piled at my back. I felt a little like an invalid. When a waitress in a starched, white dress approached, I had the sensation for a moment that she had come to take my temperature.

In the pastry cases were *tarte aux poire* and *gâteau moka, profiteroles* and *bande de tarte aux fruits, éclairs* and *entremets au chocolat, petits fours* and *génoise à la crème anglaise.* Not a baklava in sight.

The piece of *tarte* I was given was so large, I thought there had been a mistake. "I wanted just one slice," I told the waitress.

"That *is* one slice," she said.

She reached for her matches and lighted the candles on my table. A rose floated in a bowl of water in front of me. This repast was taking on the tone of a religious service.

The voice of Edith Piaf issued from a loudspeaker as the woman at the cash register leafed through a copy of *This Year's Bride.*

A woman in a long, red gown swept into the room and inclined her head graciously as she passed my table. A bell around her neck jingled when she seated herself. She ordered an éclair, which she ate after dipping it in coffee. A cigarette lay smoking in her saucer. The white rose in her hair made her look quite raffish. She must have been all of eighty.

The only others here were two couples from Germany. Sitting with their hands cupping their chins, they seemed to agree on everything.

"I loved the Blue Mosque," said one of the men. He was dressed in a cream-colored suit.

"So did I," said the woman beside him, drawing around her a shawl.

"Didn't you find Topkapi just a bit too big?" said the other man.

"*Far* too big," said the woman with the shawl. "Topkapi wore me out."

The man in the suit cleared his throat. "What I really want to know is this," he said. His tone had something desperate about it. "When exactly should you bargain?"

The other man assumed an expression comic in its gravity. "There's just one rule in Istanbul," he said. "Bargain all the time."

After the austerities of the past two months, the Pera Palas seemed overly refined. I thought fondly of Trabzon and Van and Kars. Selim had been right. Life in the hinterland is not without its rigors. But far too much is made of comfort. Anatolia did, it was true, lack Lions Clubs and Chicken McNuggets, but no one could accuse it of not being vivid.

"Believe me, gentle reader," Burton wrote about the joys of roughing it, "you will suffer real pain in returning to the turmoil of civilization. You will anticipate the bustle and the confusion of artificial life, its luxury and its false pleasures, with repugnance."

My repugnance mounted when the bill arrived. The cost of my cup of coffee and a second-rate slice of tart was a staggering ten dollars.

The Germans were talking now about Turkish guest workers.

"They invite discrimination," said the man in the cream-colored suit.

"But—" said the woman in the shawl.

"But nothing," he said. "You haven't seen them."

I have, I wanted to tell him. I have seen them in their own environment. It is on his own turf that a man deserves to be judged. Anywhere else, he is at a disadvantage. Besides, Turks overlook *our* shortcomings, don't they? When they go abroad then, shouldn't we overlook theirs?

I went outside to wait for Selim. Winter was coming on. People were wearing coats, and peddlers sold roasted chestnuts. On the Bosphorus, the ferries scuttled back and forth with their usual earnestness. But the scene gave me little pleasure. The Pera Palas had soured my mood. Istanbul was an embryonic Paris, I told myself, and for a few brief moments, it lost all its charm.

How hard my heart was then! How unyielding! All my sympathy gone. No compassion. I gazed on this city and felt nothing. An hour ago, this same scene had moved me to raptures; now it inspired indifference. No one is more pitiless than the lover brought to his senses, no one's judgment quite so harsh.

But in Istanbul one is never out of love for long. Selim turned up all agog. While I was away, he had become engaged to a German tourist. They had met when the bus they were on had braked suddenly.

"She was flung into my arms," he said.

When she tried to disengage, she couldn't. Her charm bracelet had become entangled in his Elvis button, and Selim, who prided himself on being modern, had been quick to see the significance.

"It was Kismet," he said.

Ah, that good old Eastern fatalism. It was ordained, this meeting, by a God with so much time on his hands he could arrange such things, a God who saw to it that Selim was wearing his Elvis button that day, and his fiancée her bracelet, saw to it that their bus would have to brake . . .

He stood there, beaming with happiness. And I beamed back.

"I knew you'd be happy for me," he said.

I *was* happy for him. But I was happy for me, too. He was a lot more Turkish than I'd realized. I had known him several months and thought us to be alike. But we weren't. He had been shaped by his culture more than he knew. He might claim to have European instincts, but part of him was resolutely Eastern. I thought of Van and its gleaming main street and the narrow alleyways running off it into Asia. A lot of Turks were like that, too.

Which shouldn't surprise. History is not so malleable that decrees can erase it any more than acts of parliament can reverse the habits of centuries. "Immutability is the most striking characteristic of the East," wrote Eliot Warburton over a century ago. It still is. In Turkey, the past reminds one of those alkaline batteries advertised on television: it just keeps going and going and going. . . .

It is customary to speak of westernization as having made Turkey *two* nations: one modern, the other primitive. But this suggests too neat a dichotomy. Most of the time, Turkey is modern *and* primitive. Simultaneously! Like the girl in the Moslem head scarf wearing a pair of designer glasses; or the old woman with a cordless phone sitting in a house so ancient, it seemed to be tottering.

This duality is especially marked in Istanbul. Here, past and present are like chemical compounds that repel each other even as they attract, becoming finally hard to tell apart. Here, in the midst of all those car phones, one can still watch gypsies cavort with bears. Here, in a city whose middle classes seem better acquainted with Paris than they are with Ankara, there is still the spice market—a place of such bewitching fragrance that its pigeons, it is said, are permanently drunk. Here, surrounded by traffic as dense and murderous as any in the world, it is still possible when dusk settles and the din subsides to withdraw to a cypress copse and listen to the nightingales.

Istanbul can boast many of the features of a modern metropolis—traffic jams, a housing shortage, rising crime—but, for all that, this is far from being a modern place. Using the telephone is unpredictable at best; and for all the talk of generating capacity, electricity is often in short supply. The city's twentieth-century appurtenances are so much surface trickery. Beneath it all beats a medieval heart.

Ataturk did not succeed in breaking with the past. A despot in a long line of despots, he was himself a medieval figure. A sultan in modern dress. No, the continuities are everywhere and daily grow more obvious. "The peasant is master of this country," said Ataturk, and events may prove him right. Istanbul is filling with immigrants from Anatolia—veiled women trailing after men still covered with the dust of Asia. As some in Istanbul talk of making this city an integral part of the West, the peasant is making it an integral part of the East.

Turkey *will* change. It may even become better off. But the changes will be superficial. To change substantially, it would first have to stop being fatalistic. And there's little chance of that. Not for a while.

"When are you going to marry that German woman?" I asked Selim.

He shrugged. "That depends on a lot of things," he said. "Who knows what the future holds?"

VINTAGE DEPARTURES

Available at your bookstore or call toll-free to order: 1-800-733-3000.
Credit cards only. Prices subject to change.